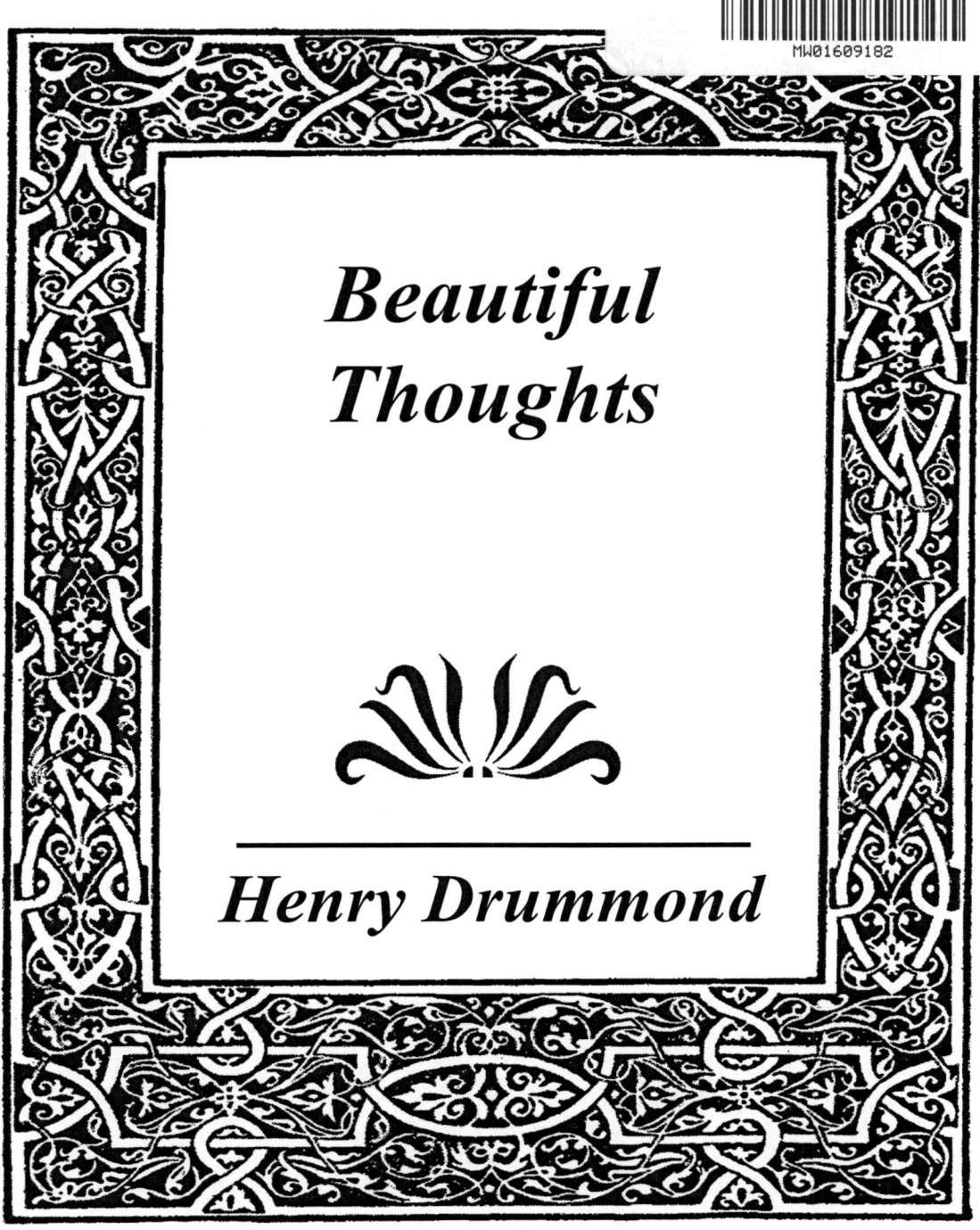

Beautiful Thoughts

Henry Drummond

1892

Beautiful Thoughts

*The invisible things of God from the
creation of the world are clearly seen,
being understood by the things
that are made.—Rom. i. 20.*

To My Dear Friend
Helen M. Archibald
This Book
Is Affectionately Inscribed.

Preface

MY first thought of writing out this little book of brief selections sprang from the desire to assist a dear friend to enjoy the Author's helpful books.

The epigrammatic style lends itself to quotation. Taste of the spring brings the traveller back to the same fountain on a day of greater leisure. Many times these "Beautiful Thoughts" have enlightened my darkness, and I send them forth with a hope and prayer that they may find echo in other hearts. E. C.

January 1st. Christianity wants nothing so much in the world as sunny people, and the old are hungrier for love than for bread, and the Oil of Joy is very cheap, and if you can help the poor on with a Garment of Praise it will be better for them than blankets. The Programme of Christianity, p. 33.

January 2d. No one who knows the content of Christianity, or feels the universal need of a Religion, can stand idly by while the intellect of his age is slowly divorcing itself from it. Natural Law, Preface, p. 22

January 3d. A Science without mystery is unknown; a Religion without mystery is absurd. However far the scientific method may penetrate the Spiritual World, there will always remain a region to be explored by a scientific faith. Natural Law, Introduction, p. 28.

January 4th. Among the mysteries which compass the world beyond, none is greater than how there can be in store for man a work more wonderful, a life more God-like than this. The Programme of Christianity, p. 62.

January 5th. The Spiritual Life is the gift of the Living Spirit. The spiritual man is no mere development of the Natural man. He is a New Creation born from Above. Natural Law, Bio-genesis, p. 65.

January 6th. Love is success, Love is happiness, Love is life. God is Love. Therefore LOVE. The Greatest Thing in the World.

January 7th. Give me the Charity which delights not in exposing the weakness of others, but "covereth all things." The Greatest Thing in the World.

January 8th. There is a sense of solidity about a Law of Nature which belongs to nothing else in the world. Here, at last, amid all that is shifting, is one thing sure; one thing outside ourselves, unbiassed, unprejudiced, uninfluenced by like or dislike, by doubt or fear. . . . This more than anything else makes one eager to see the Reign of Law traced in the Spiritual Sphere. Natural Law, Preface, p. 23.

January 9th. With Nature as the symbol of all of harmony and beauty that is known to man, must we still talk of the supernatural, not as a convenient word, but as a different order of world, . . . where the Reign of Mystery supersedes the Reign of Law? Natural Law, Introduction, p. 6.

January 10th. The Reign of Law has gradually crept into every department of Nature, transforming knowledge everywhere into Science. The process goes on, and Nature slowly appears to us as one great unity, until the borders of the Spiritual World are reached. Natural Law, Introduction, p. 13.

January 11th. No single fact in Science has ever discredited a fact in Religion. Natural Law, Introduction, p. 30.

January 12th. I shall never rise to the point of view which wishes to "raise" faith to knowledge. To me, the way of truth is to come through the knowledge of my ignorance to the submissiveness of faith, and then, making that my starting-place, to raise my knowledge into faith. Natural Law, Introduction, p. 28. Quotation from Beck: Bib. Psychol.

January 13th. If the purification of Religion comes from Science, the purification of Science, in a deeper sense, shall come from Religion. Natural Law, Introduction, p. 31.

January 14th. With the demonstration of the naturalness of the supernatural, scepticism even may come to be regarded as unscientific. And those who have wrestled long for a few bare truths to ennoble life and rest their souls in thinking of the future will not be left in doubt. Natural Law, Introduction, p. 32.

January 15th. The religion of Jesus has probably always suffered more from those who have misunderstood than from those who have opposed it. Natural Law, Bio-genesis, p. 67.

January 16th. It is impossible to believe that the amazing successions of revelations in the domain of Nature, during the last few centuries, at which the world has all but grown tired wondering, are to yield nothing for the higher life. Natural Law, Introduction, p. 32.

January 17th. Is life not full of opportunities for learning love? Every man and woman every day has a thousand of them. Greatest Thing in the World.

January 18th. What is Science but what the Natural World has said to natural men? What is Revelation but what the Spiritual World has said to Spiritual men? Natural Law, Bio-genesis, p. 73.

January 19th. Life depends upon contact with Life. It cannot spring up out of itself. It cannot develop out of anything that is not Life. There is no Spontaneous Generation in religion any more than in Nature. Christ is the source of Life in the Spiritual World; and he that hath the Son hath Life, and he that hath not the Son, whatever else he may have, hath not Life. Natural Law, Bio-genesis, p. 74.

January 20th. It is a wonderful thing that here and there in this hard, uncharitable world, there should still be left a few rare souls who think no evil. Greatest Thing in the World.

January 21st. The physical Laws may explain the inorganic world; the biological Laws may account for the development of the organic. But of the point where they meet, of that strange borderland between the dead and the living, Science is silent. It is as if God had placed everything in earth and heaven in the hands of Nature, but reserved a point at the genesis of Life for His direct appearing. Natural Law, Bio-genesis, p. 69.

January 22d. Except a mineral be born "from above"--from the Kingdom just ABOVE it--it cannot enter the Kingdom just above it. And except a man be born "from above," by the same law, he cannot enter the Kingdom just above him. Natural Law, Bio-genesis, p. 72.

January 23d. If we try to influence or elevate others, we shall soon see that success is in proportion to their belief of our belief in them. Greatest Thing in the World.

January 24th. The world is not a play-ground; it is a school-room. Life is not a holiday, but an education. And the one eternal lesson for us all is how better we can love. Greatest Thing in the World.

January 25th What a noble gift it is, the power of playing upon the souls and wills of men, and rousing them to lofty purposes and holy deeds. Greatest Thing in the World.

January 26th. The test of Religion, the final test of Religion, is not Religiousness, but Love. Greatest Thing in the World.

January 27th. There are not two laws of Bio-genesis, one for the natural, the other for the Spiritual; one law is for both. Where-ever there is Life, Life of any kind, this same law holds. Natural Law, Bio-genesis, p. 75.

January 28th. The first step in peopling these worlds with the appropriate living forms is virtually miracle. Nor in one case is there less of mystery in the act than in the other. The second birth is scarcely less perplexing to the theologian than the first to the embryologist. Natural Law, Bio-genesis, p. 76.

January 29th. There may be cases--they are probably in the majority-- where the moment of contact with the Living Spirit, though sudden, has been obscure. But the real moment and the conscious moment are two different things. Science pronounces nothing as to the conscious moment. If it did, it would probably say that that was seldom the real moment-- The moment of birth in the natural world is not a conscious moment--we do not know we are born till long afterward. Natural Law, Bio-genesis, p. 93.

January 30th. The stumbling-block to most minds is perhaps less the mere existence of the unseen than the want of definition, the apparently hopeless vagueness, and not least, the delight in this vagueness as mere vagueness by some who look upon this as the mark of quality in Spiritual things. It will be at least something to tell earnest seekers that the Spiritual World is not a castle in the air, of an architecture unknown to earth or heaven, but a fair ordered realm furnished with many familiar things and ruled by well-remembered Laws. Natural Law, Introduction, p. 26.

January 31st. Character grows in the stream of the world's life. That chiefly is where men are to learn love.

The Greatest Thing in the World.

February 1st. If a man does not exercise his arm he develops no biceps muscle; and if a man does not exercise his soul, he acquires no muscle in his soul, no strength of character, no vigour of moral fibre, nor beauty of Spiritual growth. The Greatest Thing in the World.

February 2d. A Religion without mystery is an absurdity. Even Science has its mysteries, none more inscrutable than around this Science of Life. It taught us sooner or later to expect mystery, and now we enter its domain. Let it be carefully marked, however, that the cloud does not fall and cover us till we have ascertained the most momentous truth of Religion-- that Christ is in the Christian. Natural Law, Bio-genesis, p. 88.

February 3d. Religion in having mystery is in analogy with all around it. Where there is exceptional mystery in the Spiritual World it will generally be found that there is a corresponding mystery in the natural world. Natural Law, Bio-genesis, p. 91.

February 4th. Even to earnest minds the difficulty of grasping the truth at all has always proved extreme. Philosophically, one scarcely sees either the necessity or the possibility of being born again. Why a virtuous man should not simply grow better and better until in his own right he enter the Kingdom of God is what thousands honestly and seriously fail to understand. Natural Law, Bio-genesis, p. 80.

February 5th. Lavish Love upon our equals, where it is very difficult, and for whom perhaps we each do least of all. The Greatest Thing in the World.

February 6th. Spiritual Life is not something outside ourselves. The idea is not that Christ is in heaven and that we can stretch out some mysterious faculty and deal with Him there. This is the vague form in which many conceive the truth, but it is contrary to Christ's teaching and to the analogy of nature. Life is definite and resident; and Spiritual Life is not a visit from a force, but a resident tenant in the soul. Natural Law, Bio-genesis, p. 87.

February 7th. If we neglect almost any of the domestic animals, they will rapidly revert to wild and worthless forms. Now, the same thing exactly would happen in the case of you or me. Why should man be an exception to any of the laws of nature? Natural Law, Degeneration, p. 99.

February 8th. The law of Reversion to Type runs through all creation. If a man neglect himself for a few years he will change into a worse and a lower man. If it is his body that he neglects, he will deteriorate into a wild and bestial savage.... If it is his mind, it will degenerate into imbecility and madness.... If he neglect his conscience, it will run off into lawlessness and vice. Or, lastly, if it is his soul, it must inevitably atrophy, drop off in ruin and decay. Natural Law, Degeneration, p. 99.

February 9th. Three possibilities of life, according to Science, are open to all living organisms--Balance, Evolution, and Degeneration. Natural Law, Degeneration, p. 100.

February 10th. The life of Balance is difficult. It lies

on the verge of continual temptation, its perpetual adjustments become fatiguing, its measured virtue is monotonous and uninspiring. Natural Law, Degeneration, p. 101.

February 11th. More difficult still, apparently, is the life of ever upward growth. Most men attempt it for a time, but growth is slow; and despair overtakes them while the goal is far away. Natural Law, Degeneration, p. 101.

February 12th. Degeneration is easy. Why is it easy? Why but that already in each man's very nature this principle is supreme? He feels within his soul a silent drifting motion impelling him downward with irresistible force. Natural Law, Degeneration, p. 101.

February 13th. This is Degeneration--that principle by which the organism, failing to develop itself, failing even to keep what it has got, deteriorates, and becomes more and more adapted to a degraded form of life. Natural Law, Degeneration, p. 101.

February 14th. It is a distinct fact by itself, which we can hold and examine separately, that on purely natural principles the soul that is left to itself unwatched, uncultivated, unredeemed, must fall away into death by its own nature. Natural Law, Degeneration, p. 104.

February 15th. If a man find the power of sin furiously at work within him, dragging his whole life downward to destruction, there is only one way to escape his fate--to take resolute hold of the upward power, and be borne by it to the opposite goal. Natural Law, Degeneration, p. 108.

February 16th. Neglect does more for the soul than make it miss salvation. It despoils it of its capacity for salvation. Natural Law, Degeneration, p. 110.

February 17th. Give pleasure. Lose no chance in giving pleasure. For that is the ceaseless and anonymous triumph of a truly loving spirit. Greatest Thing in the World.

February 18th. If there were uneasiness there might be hope. If there were, somewhere about our soul, a something which was not gone to sleep like all the rest; if there were a contending force anywhere; if we would let even that work instead of neglecting it, it would gain strength from hour to hour, and waken up, one at a time, each torpid and dishonoured faculty, till our whole nature became alive with strivings against self, and every avenue was open wide for God. Natural Law, Degeneration, p. 112.

February 19th. Where is the capacity for heaven to come from if it be not developed on earth? Where, indeed, is even the smallest appreciation of God and heaven to come from when so little of spirituality has ever been known or manifested here? Natural Law, Degeneration, p. 116.

February 20th. Men tell us sometimes there is no such thing as an atheist. There must be. There are some men to whom it is true that there is no God. They cannot see God because they have no eye. They have only an abortive organ, atrophied by neglect. Natural Law, Degeneration, p. 115.

February 21st. Escape means nothing more than the gradual emergence of the higher being from the lower, and nothing less. It means the gradual putting off of all that cannot enter the higher state, or heaven, and simultaneously the putting on of Christ. It involves the slow completing of the soul and the development of the capacity for God. Natural Law, Degeneration, p. 117.

February 22d. If, then, escape is to be open to us, it is not to come to us somehow, vaguely. We are not to hope for anything startling or mysterious. It is a definite opening along certain lines which are definitely marked by God, which begin at the Cross of Christ, and lead direct to Him. Natural Law, Degeneration, p. 117.

February 23d. Each man, in the silence of his own soul, must work out this salvation for himself with fear and trembling--with fear, realizing the momentous issues of his task; with trembling, lest, before the tardy work be done, the voice of Death should summon him to stop. Natural Law, Degeneration, p. 118.

February 24th. So cultivate the soul that all its powers will open out to God, and in beholding God be drawn away from sin. Natural Law, Degeneration, p. 118.

February 25th. There is a Sense of Sight in the religious nature. Neglect this, leave it undeveloped, and you never miss it. You simply see nothing. But develop it and you see God. Natural Law, Degeneration, p. 118.

February 26th. Become pure in heart. The pure in heart shall see God. Here, then, is one opening for soul-culture--the avenue through purity of heart to the spiritual seeing of God. Natural Law, Degeneration, p. 119.

February 27th. There is a Sense of Sound. Neglect this, leave it undeveloped, and you never miss it. Develop it, and you hear God. And the line along which to develop it is known to us. Obey Christ. Natural Law, Degeneration, p. 119.

February 28th He who loves will rejoice in the Truth, rejoice not in what he has been taught to believe; not in this Church's doctrine or in that; not in this issue, or in that issue; but "in the Truth." He will accept only what is real; he will strive to get at facts; he will search for Truth with a humble and unbiassed mind, and cherish whatever he finds at any sacrifice. The Greatest Thing in the World.

March 1st. "Consider the lilies of the field how they grow." Christ made the lilies and He made me--both on the same broad principle. Both together, man and flower . . .; but as men are dull at studying themselves. He points to this companion-phenomenon to teach us how to live a free and natural life, a life which God will unfold for us, without our anxiety, as He unfolds the flower. Natural Law, Growth, p. 123.

March 2d. Our efforts after Christian growth seem only a succession of failures, and, instead of rising into the beauty of holiness, our life is a daily heart-break and humiliation. Natural Law, Growth, p. 125.

March 3d. The lilies grow, Christ says, of themselves; they toil not, neither do they spin. They grow, that is, automatically, spontaneously, without trying, without fretting, without thinking. Natural Law, Growth, p. 126.

March 4th. Violent efforts to grow are right in earnestness, but wholly wrong in principle. There is but one principle of growth both for the natural and spiritual, for animal and plant, for body and soul. For all growth is an organic thing. And the principle of growing in grace is once more this, "Consider the lilies how they grow." Natural Law, Growth, p. 125.

March 5th. Earnest souls who are attempting sanctification by struggle, instead of sanctification by faith, might be spared much humiliation by learning the botany of the Sermon on the Mount. Natural Law, Growth, p. 127.

March 6th. There is only one thing greater than happiness in the world, and that is holiness; and it is not in our keeping; but what God HAS put in our power is the happiness of those about us, and that is largely to be secured by our being kind to them. The Greatest Thing in the World.

March 7th. We have all felt the brazenness of words without emotion, the hollowness, the unaccountable unpersuasiveness of eloquence behind which lies no love. The Greatest Thing in the World.

March 8th. Patience; kindness; generosity; humility; courtesy; unselfishness; good-temper; guilelessness; sincerity--these make up the supreme gift, the stature of the perfect man. The Greatest Thing in the World.

March 9th. We hear much of love to God; Christ spoke much of love to man. We make a great deal of peace with heaven; Christ spoke much of peace on earth. The Greatest Thing in the World.

March 10th. If God is spending work upon a Christian, let him be still and know that it is God. And if he wants work, he will find it there--in the being still. Natural Law, Growth, p. 137.

March 11th. If the amount of energy lost in trying

to grow were spent in fulfilling rather the conditions of growth, we should have many more cubits to show for our stature. Natural Law, Growth, p. 137.

March 12th. The conditions of growth, then, and the inward principle of growth being both supplied by Nature, the thing man has to do, the little junction left for him to complete, is to apply the one to the other. He manufactures nothing; he earns nothing; he need be anxious for nothing; his one duty is to be IN these conditions, to abide in them, to allow grace to play over him, to be still and know that this is God. Natural Law, Growth, p. 138.

March 13th. A man will often have to wrestle with his God--but not for growth. The Christian life is a composed life. The Gospel is Peace. Yet the most anxious people in the world are Christians--Christians who misunderstand the nature of growth. Life is a perpetual self-condemning because they are not growing. Natural Law, Growth, p. 139.

March 14th. All the work of the world is merely a taking advantage of energies already there. Natural Law, Growth, p. 140.

March 15th. Religion is not a strange or added thing; but the inspiration of the secular life, the breathing of an eternal spirit through this temporal world. The Greatest Thing in the World.

March 16th. The stature of the Lord Jesus was not itself reached by work, and he who thinks to approach its mystical height by anxious effort is really receding from it. Natural Law, Growth, p. 127.

March 17th. For the Life must develop out according to its type; and being a germ of the Christ-life, it must unfold into a Christ. Natural Law, Growth, p. 129.

March 18th. The sneer at the godly man for his imperfections is ill-judged. A blade is a small thing. At first it grows very near the earth. It is often soiled and crushed and downtrodden. But it is a living thing,...and "it doth not yet appear what it shall be." Natural Law, Growth, p. 129.

March 19th. Christ's protest is not against work, but against anxious thought. Natural Law, Growth, p. 136.

March 20th. If God is adding to our spiritual stature, unfolding the new nature within us, it is a mistake to keep twitching at the petals with our coarse fingers. We must seek to let the Creative Hand alone. "It is God which giveth the increase." Natural Law, Growth, p. 137.

March 21st. Love is PATIENCE. This is the normal attitude of Love; Love passive, Love waiting to begin; not in a hurry; calm; ready to do its work when the summons comes, but meantime wearing the ornament of a meek and quiet spirit. The Greatest Thing in the World.

March 22d. Have you ever noticed how much of Christ's life was spent in doing kind things? The Greatest Thing in the World.

March 23d. I wonder why it is we are not all kinder than we are! How much the world needs it. How easily it is done. How instantaneously it acts. How infallibly it is remembered. How superabundantly it pays itself back --for there is no debtor in the world so honourable, so superbly honourable as Love. The Greatest Thing in the

World.

March 24th. To love abundantly is to live abundantly, and to love forever is to live forever. Hence, eternal life is inextricably bound up with love. The Greatest Thing in the World.

March 25th. Man is a mass of correspondences, and because of these, because he is alive to countless objects and influences to which lower organisms are dead, he is the most living of all creatures. Natural Law, Death, p. 155.

March 26th. All organisms are living and dead--living to all within the circumference of their correspondences, dead to all beyond. . . . Until man appears there is no organism to correspond with the whole environment. Natural Law, Death, p. 155.

March 27th. Is man in correspondence with the whole environment or is he not? . . . He is not. Of men generally it cannot be said that they are in living contact with that part of the environment which is called the spiritual world. Natural Law, Death, p. 156.

March 28th. The animal world and the plant world are the same world. They are different parts of one environment. And the natural and spiritual are likewise one. Natural Law, Death, p. 157.

March 29th. What we have correspondence with, that we call natural; what we have little or no correspondence with, that we call Spiritual. Natural Law, Death, p. 157.

March 30th. Those who are in communion with God live, those who are not are dead. Natural Law, Death, p.

158.

March 31st. This earthly mind may be of noble calibre, enriched by culture, high-toned, virtuous, and pure. But if it know not God? What though its correspondences reach to the stars of heaven or grasp the magnitudes of Time and Space? The stars of heaven are not heaven. Space is not God. Natural Law, Death, p. 158.

April 1st. We do not picture the possessor of this carnal mind as in any sense a monster. We have said he may be high-toned, virtuous, and pure. The plant is not a monster because it is dead to the voice of the bird; nor is he a monster who is dead to the voice of God. The contention at present simply is that he is DEAD. Natural Law, Death, p. 159.

April 2d. What is the creed of the Agnostic, but the confession of the spiritual numbness of humanity? Natural Law, Death, p. 160.

April 3d. The nescience of the Agnostic philosophy is the proof from experience that to be carnally minded is Death. Natural Law, p. 161.

April 4th. The Christian apologist never further misses the mark than when he refuses the testimony of the Agnostic to himself. When the Agnostic tells me he is blind and deaf, dumb, torpid, and dead to the spiritual world, I must believe him. Jesus tells me that. Paul tells me that. Science tells me that. He knows nothing of this outermost circle; and we are compelled to trust his sincerity as readily when he deplores it as if, being a man without an ear, he professed to know nothing of a musical world, or being without taste, of a world of art. Natural Law, Death, p. 160.

April 5th. It brings no solace to the unspiritual man to be told he is mistaken. To say he is self-deceived is neither to compliment him nor Christianity. He builds in all sincerity who raises his altar to the UNKNOWN God. He does not know God. With all his marvellous and complex correspondences, he is still one correspondence short. Natural Law, Death, p. 161.

April 6th. Only one thing truly need the Christian envy, the large, rich, generous soul which "envieth not." The Greatest Thing in the World.

April 7th. Whenever you attempt a good work you will find other men doing the same kind of work, and probably doing it better. Envy them not. The Greatest Thing in the World.

April 8th. I say that man believes in a God, who feels himself in the presence of a Power which is not himself, and is immeasurably above himself, a Power in the contemplation of which he is absorbed, in the knowledge of which he finds safety and happiness. Natural Law, Death, p. 162.

April 9th. What men deny is not a God. It is the correspondence. The very confession of the Unknowable is itself the dull recognition of an Environment beyond themselves, and for which they feel they lack the correspondence. It is this want that makes their God the Unknown God. And it is this that makes them DEAD. Natural Law, Death, p. 163.

April 10th. God is not confined to the outermost circle of environment, He lives and moves and has His being in the whole. Those who only seek Him in the further zone can only find a part. The Christian who knows not God in Nature, who does not, that is to say, correspond with the whole environment, most certainly is partially dead. Natural Law, Death, p. 163.

April 11th. After you have been kind, after Love has stolen forth into the world and done its beautiful work, go back into the shade again and say nothing about it. The Greatest Thing in the World.

April 12th. The absence of the true Light means moral Death. The darkness of the natural world to the intellect is not all. What history testifies to is, first the partial, and then the total eclipse of virtue that always follows the abandonment of belief in a personal God. Natural Law, Death, p. 167.

April 13th. The only greatness is unselfish love....There is a great difference between TRYING TO PLEASE and GIVING PLEASURE. The Greatest Thing in the World.

April 14th. The conception of a God gives an altogether new colour to worldliness and vice. Worldliness it changes into heathenism, vice into blasphemy. The carnal mind, the mind which is turned away from God, which will not correspond with God--this is not moral only but spiritual Death. And Sin, that which separates from God, which disobeys God, which CAN not in that state correspond with God--this is hell. Natural Law, Death, p. 169.

April 15th. If sin is estrangement from God, this very

estrangement is Death. It is a want of correspondence. If sin is selfishness, it is conducted at the expense of life. Its wages are Death--"he that loveth his life," said Christ, "shall lose it." Natural Law, Death, p. 170.

April 16th. Obviously if the mind turns away from one part of the environment it will only do so under some temptation to correspond with another. This temptation, at bottom, can only come from one source--the love of self. The irreligious man's correspondences are concentrated upon himself. He worships himself. Self-gratification rather than self-denial; independence rather than submission--these are the rules of life. And this is at once the poorest and the commonest form of idolatry. Natural Law, p. 170.

April 17th. You will find . . . that the people who influence you are people who believe in you. The Greatest Thing in the World.

April 18th. The development of any organism in any direction is dependent on its environment. A living cell cut off from air will die. A seed-germ apart from moisture and an appropriate temperature will make the ground its grave for centuries. Human nature, likewise, is subject to similar conditions. It can only develop in presence of its environment. No matter what its possibilities may be, no matter what seeds of thought or virtue, what germs of genius or of art, lie latent in its breast, until the appropriate environment present itself the correspondence is denied, the development discouraged, the most splendid possibilities of life remain unrealized, and thought and virtue, genius and art, are dead. Natural Law, p. 171.

April 19th. The true environment of the moral life is God. Here conscience wakes. Here kindles love. Duty here becomes heroic; and that righteousness begins to live which alone is to live forever. But if this Atmosphere is not, the dwarfed soul must perish for mere want of its native air. And its Death is a strictly natural Death. It is not an exceptional judgment upon Atheism. In the same circumstances, in the same averted relation to their environment, the poet, the musician, the artist, would alike perish to poetry, to music, and to art. Natural Law, p. 171.

April 20th. Every environment is a cause. Its effect upon me is exactly proportionate to my correspondence with it. If I correspond with part of it, part of myself is influenced. If I correspond with more, more of myself is influenced; if with all, all is influenced. If I correspond with the world, I become worldly; if with God, I become Divine. Natural Law, Death, p. 171.

April 21st. You can dwarf a soul just as you can dwarf a plant, by depriving it of a full environment. Such a soul for a time may have a "name to live." Its character may betray no sign of atrophy. But its very virtue somehow has the pallor of a flower that is grown in darkness, or as the herb which has never seen the sun, no fragrance breathes from its spirit. Natural Law, p. 173.

April 22d. I shall pass through this world but once. Any good thing, therefore, that I can do, or any kindness that I can show to any human being, let me do it now. Let me not defer it or neglect it, for I shall not pass this way again.

The Greatest Thing in the World.

April 23d. There is no happiness in having and getting, but only in giving . . . half the world is on the wrong scent in the pursuit of happiness. The Greatest Thing in the World.

April 24th. No form of vice, not worldliness, not greed of gold, not drunkenness itself, does more to un-Christianize society than evil temper. The Greatest Thing in the World.

April 25th. How many prodigals are kept out of the Kingdom of God by the unlovely character of those who profess to be inside! The Greatest Thing in the World.

April 26th. A want of patience, a want of kindness, a want of generosity, a want of courtesy, a want of unselfishness, are all instantaneously symbolized in one flash of Temper. The Greatest Thing in the World.

April 27th. Souls are made sweet not by taking the acid fluids out, but by putting something in--a great Love, a new Spirit--the Spirit of Christ. The Greatest Thing in the World.

April 28th. Christ, the Spirit of Christ, interpenetrating ours, sweetens, purifies, transforms all. This only can eradicate what is wrong, work a chemical change, renovate and regenerate, and rehabilitate the inner man. Willpower does not change men. Time does not change men. Christ does. The Greatest Thing in the World.

April 29th Guilelessness is the grace for suspicious people. And the possession of it is the great secret of personal influence. You will find, if you think for a moment, that the people who influence you are people who believe in you. In an atmosphere of suspicion men shrivel up; but in that atmosphere they expand, and find encouragement and educative fellowship. The Greatest Thing in the World.

April 30th. Do not quarrel . . . with your lot in life. Do not complain of its never-ceasing cares, its petty environment, the vexations you have to stand, the small and sordid souls you have to live and work with. The Greatest Thing in the World.

May 1st. The moment the new life is begun there comes a genuine anxiety to break with the old. For the former environment has now become embarrassing. It refuses its dismissal from consciousness. It competes doggedly with the new Environment for a share of the correspondences. And in a hundred ways the former traditions, the memories and passions of the past, the fixed associations and habits of the earlier life, now complicate the new relation. The complex and bewildered soul, in fact, finds itself in correspondence with two environments, each with urgent but yet incompatible claims. It is a dual soul living in a double world, a world whose inhabitants are deadly enemies, and engaged in perpetual civil war. Natural Law, Mortification, p. 179.

May 2d. How can the New Life deliver itself from the still-persistent past? A ready solution of the difficulty would be TO DIE. . . . If we cannot die altogether, . . . the most we can do is to die as much as we can. . . . To die to any environment is to withdraw correspondence with it, to cut ourselves off, so far as possible, from all communication with it. So that the solution of the problem will simply be this, for the spiritual life to reverse continuously the processes of the natural life. Natural Law, Mortification, p. 180.

May 3d. The spiritual man having passed from Death unto Life, the natural man must next proceed to pass from Life unto Death. Having opened the new set of correspondences, he must deliberately close up the old. Regeneration in short must be accompanied by Degeneration. Natural Law, Mortification, p. 181.

May 4th. The peculiar feature of Death by Suicide is that it is not only self-inflicted but sudden. And there are many sins which must either be dealt with suddenly or not at all. Natural Law, Mortification, p. 183.

May 5th. If the Christian is to "live unto God," he must "die unto sin." If he does not kill sin, sin will inevitably kill him. Recognizing this, he must set himself to reduce the number of his correspondences-- retaining and developing those which lead to a fuller life, unconditionally withdrawing those which in any way tend in an opposite direction. This stoppage of correspondences is a voluntary act, a crucifixion of the flesh, a suicide. Natural Law, Mortification, p. 182.

May 6th. Do not resent temptation; do not be perplexed because it seems to thicken round you more and more, and ceases neither for effort nor for agony nor prayer. That is your practice. That is the practice which God appoints you; and it is having its work in making you patient, and humble, and generous, and unselfish, and kind, and courteous. The Greatest Thing in the World.

May 7th. It is a peculiarity of the sinful state, that as a general rule men are linked to evil mainly by a single correspondence. Few men break the whole law. Our natures, fortunately, are not large enough to make us guilty of all, and the restraints of circumstances are usually such as to leave a loophole in the life of each individual for only a single habitual sin. But it is very easy to see how this reduction of our intercourse with evil to a single correspondence blinds us to our true position. Natural Law, Mortification, p. 186.

May 8th. One little weakness, we are apt to fancy, all men must be allowed, and we even claim a certain indulgence for that apparent necessity of nature which we call our besetting sin. Yet to break with the lower environment at all, to many, is to break at this single point. Natural Law, p. 186.

May 9th. There may be only one avenue between the new life and the old, it may be but a small and SUBTERRANEAN PASSAGE, but this is sufficient to keep the old life in. So long as that remains the victim is not "dead unto sin," and therefore he cannot "live unto God." Natural Law, p. 187.

May 10th. Do not grudge the hand that is moulding the still too shapeless image within you. It is growing more beautiful, though you see it not, and every touch of temptation may add to its perfection. Therefore keep in the midst of life. Do not isolate yourself. Be among men, and among things, and among troubles, and difficulties, and obstacles. The Greatest Thing in the World.

May 11th. Contemplate the love of Christ, and you will love. Stand before that mirror, reflect Christ's character, and you will be changed into the same image from tenderness to tenderness. There is no other way. You cannot love to order. You can only look at the lovely object, and fall in love with it, and grow into likeness to it. The Greatest Thing in the World.

May 12th. In the natural world it only requires a single vital correspondence of the body to be out of order to ensure Death. It is not necessary to have consumption, diabetes, and an aneurism to bring the body to the grave, if it have heart disease. He who is fatally diseased in one organ necessarily pays the penalty with his life, though all the others be in perfect health. And such, likewise, are the mysterious unity and correlation of functions in the spiritual organism that the disease of one member may involve the ruin of the whole. Natural Law, Mortification, p. 187.

May 13th. To break altogether, and at every point, with the old environment, is a simple impossibility. So long as the regenerate man is kept in this world he must find the old environment at many points a severe temptation. Natural Law, Mortification, p. 190.

May 14th. Power over very many of the commonest temptations is only to be won by degrees, and however anxious one might be to apply the summary method to every case, he soon finds it impossible in practice. Natural Law, Mortification, p. 190.

May 15th. The ill-tempered person . . . can make very little of his environment. However he may attempt to circumscribe it in certain directions, there will always remain a wide and ever-changing area to stimulate his irascibility. His environment, in short, is an inconstant quantity, and his most elaborate calculations and precautions must often and suddenly fail him. Natural Law, Mortification, p. 191.

May 16th. What the ill-tempered person has to deal with, . . . mainly, is the correspondence, the temper itself. And that, he well knows, involves a long and humiliating discipline. The case is not at all a surgical but a medical one, and the knife is here of no more use than in a fever. A specific irritant has poisoned his veins. And the acrid humours that are breaking out all over the surface of his life are only to be subdued by a gradual sweetening of the inward spirit. Natural Law, Mortification, p. 191.

May 17th. The man whose blood is pure has nothing to fear. So he whose spirit is purified and sweetened becomes proof against these germs of sin. "Anger, wrath, malice and railing" in such a soil can find no root. Natural Law, Mortification, p. 192.

May 18th. The Mortification of a member . . .is based on the Law of Degeneration. The useless member here is not cut off, but simply relieved as much as possible of all exercise. This encourages the gradual decay of the parts, and as it is more and more neglected it ceases to be a channel for life at all. So an organism "mortifies" its members. Natural Law, Mortification, p. 193.

May 19th. Man's spiritual life consists in the number

and fulness of his correspondences with God. In order to develop these he may be constrained to insulate them, to enclose them from the other correspondences, to shut himself in with them. In many ways the limitation of the natural life is the necessary condition of the full enjoyment of the spiritual life. Natural Law, Mortification, p. 195.

May 20th. No man is called to a life of self-denial for its own sake. It is in order to a compensation which, though sometimes difficult to see, is always real and always proportionate. No truth, perhaps, in practical religion is more lost sight of. We cherish somehow a lingering rebellion against the doctrine of self-denial--as if our nature, or our circumstances, or our conscience, dealt with us severely in loading us with the daily cross. But is it not plain after all that the life of self-denial is the more abundant life--more abundant just in proportion to the ampler crucifixion of the narrower life? Is it not a clear case of exchange--an exchange, however, where the advantage is entirely on our side? We give up a correspondence in which there is a little life to enjoy a correspondence in which there is an abundant life. What though we sacrifice a hundred such correspondences? We make but the more room for the great one that is left. Natural Law, Mortification, p. 195.

May 21st. Do not spoil your life at the outset with unworthy and impoverishing correspondences; and if it is growing truly rich and abundant, be very jealous of ever diluting its high eternal quality with anything of earth. Natural Law, Mortification, p. 196.

May 22d. To concentrate upon a few great correspondences, to oppose to the death the perpetual petty larceny of our life by trifles--these are the conditions for the highest and happiest life. . . . The penalty of evading self-denial also is just that we get the lesser instead of the larger good. The punishment of sin is inseparably bound up with itself. Natural Law, Mortification, p. 196.

May 23d. Each man has only a certain amount of life, of time, of attention--a definite measurable quantity. If he gives any of it to this life solely it is wasted. Therefore Christ says, Hate life, limit life, lest you steal your love for it from something that deserves it more. Natural Law, Mortification, p. 197.

May 24th. To refuse to deny one's self is just to be left with the self undented. When the balance of life is struck, the self will be found still there. The discipline of life was meant to destroy this self, but that discipline having been evaded--and we all to some extent have opportunities, and too often exercise them, of taking the narrow path by the shortest cuts--its purpose is baulked. But the soul is the loser. In seeking to gain its life it has really lost it. Natural Law, Mortification, p. 196.

May 25th. Suppose we deliberately made up our minds as to what things we were henceforth to allow to become our life? Suppose we selected a given area of our environment and determined once for all that our correspondences should go to that alone, fencing in this area all round with a morally impassable wall? True, to others, we should seem to live a poorer life; they would see that our environment was circumscribed, and call us narrow because it was narrow. But, well-chosen, this limited life would be really the fullest life; it would be rich in the highest and worthiest, and poor in the smallest and basest, correspondences. Natural Law, Mortification, p. 199.

May 26th. The well-defined spiritual life is not only the highest life, but it is also the most easily lived. The whole cross is more easily carried than the half. It is the man who tries to make the best of both worlds who makes nothing of either. And he who seeks to serve two masters misses the benediction of both. Natural Law, Mortification, p. 199.

May 27th. You will find, as you look back upon your life, that the moments that stand out, the moments when you have really lived, are the moments when you have done things in a spirit of love. As memory scans the past, above and beyond all the transitory pleasures of life, there leap forward those supreme hours when you have been enabled to do unnoticed kindnesses to those round about you, things too trifling to speak about, but which you feel have entered into your eternal life. The Greatest Thing in the World, p. 60.

May 28th. No man can become a saint in his sleep; and to fulfil the condition required demands a certain amount of prayer and meditation and time, just as improvement in any direction, bodily or mental, requires preparation and care. Address yourselves to that one thing; at any cost have this transcendent character exchanged for yours. The Greatest Thing in the World, p. 60.

May 29th. He who has taken his stand, who has drawn a

boundary line, sharp and deep, about his religious life, who has marked off all beyond as for ever forbidden ground to him, finds the yoke easy and the burden light. For this forbidden environment comes to be as if it were not. His faculties falling out of correspondence, slowly lose their sensibilities. And the balm of Death numbing his lower nature releases him for the scarce disturbed communion of a higher life. So even here to die is gain. Natural Law, Mortification, p. 199.

May 30th. Remain side by side with Him who loved us, and gave Himself for us, and you too will become a permanent magnet, a permanently attractive force; and like Him you will draw all men unto you, like Him you will be drawn unto all men. That is the inevitable effect of Love. Any man who fulfils that cause must have that effect produced in him. The Greatest Thing in the World, p. 45.

May 31st. Try to give up the idea that religion comes to us by chance, or by mystery, or by caprice. It comes to us by natural law, or by supernatural law, for all law is Divine. The Greatest Thing in the World, p. 46.

June 1st. We love others, we love everybody, we love our enemies, because He first loved us....And that is how the love of God melts down the unlovely heart in man, and begets in him the new creature, who is patient and humble and gentle and unselfish. The Greatest Thing in the World, p. 46.

June 2d. The belief in Science as an aid to faith is not yet ripe enough to warrant men in searching there for witnesses to the highest Christian truths. The inspiration of Nature, it is thought, extends to the humbler doctrines alone. And yet the reverent inquirer who guides his steps in the right direction may find even now, in the still dim twilight of the scientific world, much that will illuminate and intensify his sublimest faith. Natural Law, Eternal Life, p. 204.

June 3d. Life becomes fuller and fuller, richer and richer, more and more sensitive and responsive to an ever-widening Environment as we rise in the chain of being. Natural Law, Eternal Life, p. 207.

June 4th. Before we reach an Eternal Life we must pass beyond that point at which all ordinary correspondences inevitably cease. We must find an organism so high and complex, that at some point in its development it shall have added a correspondence which organic death is powerless to arrest. Natural Law, Eternal Life, p. 213.

June 5th. Uninterrupted correspondence with a perfect Environment is Eternal Life, according to Science. "This is Life Eternal," said Christ, "that they may know Thee, the only true God, and Jesus Christ whom Thou hast sent." Life Eternal is to know God. To know God is to "correspond" with God. To correspond with God is to correspond with a Perfect Environment. And the organism which attains to this, in the nature of things, must live forever. Here is "eternal existence and eternal knowledge." Natural Law, Eternal Life, p. 215.

June 6th. To find a new Environment again and cultivate relation with it is to find a new Life. To live is to correspond, and to correspond is to live. So much is true in Science. But it is also true in Religion. And it is of great importance to observe that to Religion also the conception of Life is a correspondence. No truth of Christianity has been more ignorantly or wilfully travestied than the doctrine of Immortality. The popular idea, in spite of a hundred protests, is that Eternal Life is to live forever. ... We are told that Life Eternal is not to live. This is Life Eternal--TO KNOW. Natural Law, Eternal Life, p. 216.

June 7th. From time to time the taunt is thrown at Religion, not unseldom from lips which Science ought to have taught more caution, that the Future Life of Christianity is simply a prolonged existence, an eternal monotony, a blind and indefinite continuance of being. The Bible never could commit itself to any such empty platitude; nor could Christianity ever offer to the world a hope so colourless. Not that Eternal Life has nothing to do with everlastingness. That is part of the conception. And it is this aspect of the question that first arrests us in the field of Science. Natural Law, Eternal Life, p. 216.

June 8th. Science speaks to us indeed of much more than numbers of years. It defines degrees of Life. It explains a widening Environment. It unfolds the relation between a widening Environment and increasing complexity in organisms. And if it has no absolute contribution to the content of Religion, its analogies are not limited to a point. It yields to Immortality, and this is the most that Science can do in any case, the broad framework for a doctrine. Natural Law, Eternal Life, p. 217.

June 9th. To correspond with the God of Science,

the Eternal Unknowable, would be everlasting existence; to correspond with "the true God and Jesus Christ," is Eternal Life. The quality of the Eternal Life alone makes the heaven; mere everlastingness might be no boon. Even the brief span of the temporal life is too long for those who spend its years in sorrow. Natural Law, Eternal Life, p. 220.

June 10th. To Christianity, "he that hath the Son of God hath Life, and he that hath not the Son hath not Life." This, as we take it, defines the correspondence which is to bridge the grave. This is the clue to the nature of the Life that lies at the back of the spiritual organism. And this is the true solution of the mystery of Eternal Life. Natural Law, Eternal Life, p. 227.

June 11th. The relation between the spiritual man and his Environment is, in theological language, a filial relation. With the new Spirit, the filial correspondence, he knows the Father--and this is Life Eternal. Natural Law, Eternal Life, p. 229.

June 12th. It takes the Divine to know the Divine--but in no more mysterious sense than it takes the human to understand the human. The analogy, indeed, for the whole field here has been finely expressed already by Paul: "What man," he asks, "knoweth the things of a man, save the spirit of man which is in him? Even so the things of God knoweth no man, but the Spirit of God. Now we have received, not the spirit of the world, but the spirit which is of God; that we might know the things that are freely given to us of God."--I. Cor. ii. 11, 12. Natural Law,

Eternal Life, p. 229.

June 13th. To go outside what we call Nature is not to go outside Environment. Nature, the natural Environment, is only a part of Environment. There is another large part, which, though some profess to have no correspondence with it, is not on that account unreal, or even unnatural. The mental and moral world is unknown to the plant. But it is real. Natural Law, Eternal Life, p. 232.

June 14th. Things are natural or supernatural simply according to where one stands. Man is supernatural to the mineral; God is supernatural to the man. When a mineral is seized upon by the living plant and elevated to the organic kingdom, no trespass against Nature is committed. It merely enters a larger Environment, which before was supernatural to it, but which now is entirely natural. When the heart of a man, again, is seized upon by the quickening Spirit of God, no further violence is done to natural law. It is another case of the inorganic, so to speak, passing into the organic. Natural Law, Eternal Life, p. 232.

June 15th. Correspondence in any case is the gift of Environment. The natural Environment gives men their natural faculties; the spiritual affords them their spiritual faculties. It is natural for the spiritual Environment to supply the spiritual faculties; it would be quite unnatural for the natural Environment to do it. The natural law of Biogenesis forbids it; the moral fact that the finite cannot comprehend the Infinite is against it; the spiritual principle that flesh and blood, cannot inherit the Kingdom of God renders it absurd. Natural Law, Eternal Life, p. 233.

June 16th. Organisms are not added to by accretion, as in the case of minerals, but by growth. And the spiritual faculties are organized in the spiritual protoplasm of the soul, just as other faculties are organized in the protoplasm of the body. Natural Law, Eternal Life, p. 233.

June 17th. It ought to be placed in the forefront of all Christian teaching that Christ's mission on earth was to give men Life. "I am come," He said, "that ye might have Life, and that ye might have it more abundantly." And that He meant literal Life, literal spiritual and Eternal Life, is clear from the whole course of His teaching and acting. Natural Law, Eternal Life, p. 235.

June 18th. The effort to detect the living Spirit must be at least as idle as the attempt to subject protoplasm to microscopic examination in the hope of discovering Life. We are warned, also, not to expect too much. "Thou canst not tell whence it cometh or whither it goeth." Natural Law, Eternal Life, p. 237.

June 19th. Many men would be religious if they knew where to begin; many would be more religious if they were sure where it would end. It is not indifference that keeps some men from God, but ignorance. "Good Master, what must I do to inherit Eternal Life?" is still the deepest question of the age. Natural Law, Eternal Life, p. 237.

June 20th. The voice of God and the voice of Nature. I cannot be wrong if I listen to them. Sometimes, when uncertain of a voice from its very loudness, we catch the missing syllable in the echo. In God and Nature we have Voice and Echo. When I hear both, I am assured. My sense of hearing does not betray me twice. I recognize the Voice in the Echo, the Echo makes me certain of the Voice; I listen and I know. Natural Law, Eternal Life, p. 238.

June 21st. The soul is a living organism. And for any question as to the soul's Life we must appeal to Life-science. And what does the Life-science teach? That if I am to inherit Eternal Life, I must cultivate a correspondence with the Eternal. Natural Law, Eternal Life, p. 239.

June 22d. All knowledge lies in Environment. When I want to know about minerals I go to minerals. When I want to know about flowers I go to flowers. And they tell me. In their own way they speak to me, each in its own way, and each for itself--not the mineral for the flower, which is impossible, nor the flower for the mineral, which is also impossible. So if I want to know about Man, I go to his part of the Environment. And he tells me about himself, not as the plant or the mineral, for he is neither, but in his own way. And if I want to know about God, I go to His part of the Environment. And He tells me about Himself, not as a Man, for He is not Man, but in His own way. Natural Law, Eternal Life, p. 239.

June 23d. Just as naturally as the flower and the mineral and the Man, each in their own way, tell me about themselves, He tells me about Himself. He very strangely condescends indeed in making things plain to me, actually assuming for a time the Form of a Man that I at my poor level may better see Him. This is my opportunity to know Him. This incarnation is God making Himself accessible to human thought--God opening to Man the possibility of correspondence through Jesus Christ. Natural Law, Eternal Life, p. 240.

June 24th. Having opened correspondence with the Eternal Environment, the subsequent stages are in the line of all other normal development. We have but to continue, to deepen, to extend, and to enrich the correspondence that has been begun. And we shall soon find to our surprise that this is accompanied by another and parallel process. The action is not all upon our side. The Environment also will be found to correspond. Natural Law, Eternal Life, p. 241.

June 25th. Let us look for the influence of Environment on the spiritual nature of him who has opened correspondence with God. Reaching out his eager and quickened faculties to the spiritual world around him, shall he not become spiritual? In vital contact with Holiness, shall he not become holy? Breathing now an atmosphere of ineffable Purity, shall he miss becoming pure? Walking with God from day to day, shall he fail to be taught of God? Natural Law, Eternal Life, p. 242.

June 26th. Growth in grace is sometimes described as a strange, mystical, and unintelligible process. It is mystical, but neither strange nor unintelligible. It proceeds according to Natural Law, and the leading factor in sanctification is Influence of Environment. Natural Law, Eternal Life, p. 242.

June 27th. Will the evolutionist who admits the regeneration of the frog under the modifying influence of a continued correspondence with a new environment, care to question the possibility of the soul acquiring such a faculty as that of Prayer, the marvellous breathing-function of the new creature, when in contact with the atmosphere of a besetting God? Is the change from the earthly to the heavenly more mysterious than the change from the aquatic to the terrestrial mode of life? Is Evolution to stop with the organic? If it be objected that it has taken ages to perfect the function in the batrachian, the reply is, that it will take ages to perfect the function in the Christian. Natural Law, Eternal Life, p. 244.

June 28th. We have indeed spoken of the spiritual correspondence as already perfect--but it is perfect only as the bud is perfect. "It doth not yet appear what it shall be," any more than it appeared a million years ago what the evolving batrachian would be. Natural Law, Eternal Life, p. 244.

June 29th. In a sense, all that belongs to Time belongs also to Eternity; but these lower correspondences are in their nature unfitted for an Eternal Life. Even if they were perfect in their relation to their Environment, they would still not be Eternal. . . . An Eternal Life demands an Eternal Environment. Natural Law, Eternal Life, p. 245.

June 30th. The final preparation . . . for the inheriting of Eternal Life must consist in the abandonment of the non-eternal elements. These must be unloosed and dissociated from the higher elements, And this is effected by a closing catastrophe--Death. Natural Law, Eternal Life, p. 248.

July 1st. "Perfect correspondence," according to Mr. Herbert Spencer, would be "perfect Life." To abolish Death, therefore, all that would be necessary would be to abolish Imperfection. But it is the claim of Christianity that it can abolish Death. And it is significant to notice that it does so by meeting this very demand of Science--it abolishes Imperfection. Natural Law, Eternal Life, p. 249.

July 2d. The part of the organism which begins to get out of correspondence with the Organic Environment is the only part which is in vital correspondence with it. Though a fatal disadvantage to the natural man to be thrown out of correspondence with this Environment, it is of inestimable importance to the spiritual man. For so long as it is maintained the way is barred for a further Evolution. And hence the condition necessary for the further Evolution is that the spiritual be released from the natural. That is to say, the condition of the further Evolution is Death. Natural Law, Eternal Life, p. 249.

July 3d. The sifting of the correspondences is done by Nature. This is its last and greatest contribution to mankind. Over the mouth of the grave the perfect and the imperfect submit to their final separation. Each goes to its own--earth to earth, ashes to ashes, dust to dust, Spirit to Spirit. "The dust shall return to the earth as it was; and the Spirit shall return unto God who gave it." Natural Law, Eternal Life, p. 249.

July 4th. Few things are less understood than the conditions of the spiritual life. The distressing incompetence of which most of us are conscious in trying to work out our spiritual experience is due perhaps less to the diseased will which we commonly blame for it than to imperfect knowledge of the right conditions. It does not occur to us how natural the spiritual is. We still strive for some strange transcendent thing; we seek to promote life by methods as unnatural as they prove unsuccessful; and only the utter incomprehensibility of the whole region prevents us seeing fully--what we already half-suspect--how completely we are missing the road. Natural Law, Environment, p. 256.

July 5th. Living in the spiritual world . . . is just as simple as living in the natural world; and it is the same kind of simplicity. It is the same kind of simplicity for it is the same kind of world--there are not two kinds of worlds. The conditions of life in the one are the conditions of life in the other. And till these conditions are sensibly grasped, as the conditions of all life, it is impossible that the personal effort after the highest life should be other than a blind struggle carried on in fruitless sorrow and humiliation. Natural Law, Environment, p. 257.

July 6th. Heredity and Environment are the master-influences of the organic world. These have made all of us what we are. These forces are still ceaselessly playing upon all our lives. And he who truly understands these influences; he who has decided how much to allow to each; he who can regulate new forces as they arise, or adjust them to the old, so directing them as at one moment to make them cooperate, at another to counteract one another, understands the rationale of personal development. Natural Law, Environment, p. 255.

July 7th. To seize continuously the opportunity of

more and more perfect adjustment to better and higher conditions, to balance some inward evil with some purer influence acting from without, in a word to make our Environment at the same time that it is making us--these are the secrets of a well-ordered and successful life. Natural Law, Environment, p. 256.

July 8th. In the spiritual world . . . the subtle influences which form and transform the soul are Heredity and Environment. And here especially, where all is invisible, where much that we feel to be real is yet so ill defined, it becomes of vital practical moment to clarify the atmosphere as far as possible with conceptions borrowed from the natural life. Natural Law, Environment, p. 256.

July 9th. What Heredity has to do for us is determined outside ourselves. No man can select his own parents. But every man to some extent can choose his own Environment. His relation to it, however largely determined by Heredity in the first instance, is always open to alteration. And so great is his control over Environment and so radical its influence over him, that he can so direct it as either to undo, modify, perpetuate, or intensify the earlier hereditary influences within certain limits. Natural Law, Environment, p. 257.

July 10th. One might show how the moral man is acted upon and changed continuously by the influences, secret and open, of his surroundings, by the tone of society, by the company he keeps, by his occupation, by the books he reads, by Nature, by all, in short, that constitutes the habitual atmosphere of his thoughts and the little world of his daily choice. Or one might go deeper still and prove how the spiritual life also is modified from outside sources--its health or disease, its growth or decay, all its changes for better or for worse being determined by the varying and successive circumstances in which the religious habits are cultivated. Natural Law, Environment, p. 260.

July 11th. In the spiritual world ... he will be wise who courts acquaintance with the most ordinary and transparent facts of Nature; and in laying the foundations for a religious life he will make no unworthy beginning who carries with him an impressive sense of so obvious a truth as that without Environment there can be no life. Natural Law, Environment, p. 264.

July 12th. There is in the spiritual organism a principle of life; but that is not self-existent. It requires a second factor, a something in which to live and move and have its being, an Environment. Without this it cannot live or move or have any being. Without Environment the soul is as the carbon without the oxygen, as the fish without the water, as the animal frame without the extrinsic conditions of vitality. Natural Law, Environment, p. 264.

July 13th. What is the Spiritual Environment? It is God. Without this, therefore, there is no life, no thought, no energy, nothing---"without Me ye can do nothing." Natural Law, Environment, p. 265.

July 14th. The cardinal error in the religious life is to attempt to live without an Environment. Spiritual experience occupies itself, not too much, but too exclusively, with one factor--the soul. We delight in dissecting this much-tortured faculty, from time to time, in search of a certain something which we call our faith--forgetting that faith is but an attitude, an empty hand for grasping an environing Presence. Natural Law, Environment, p 265.

July 15th. When we feel the need of a power by which to overcome the world, how often do we not seek to generate it within ourselves by some forced process, some fresh girding of the will, some strained activity which only leaves the soul in further exhaustion? Natural Law, Environment, p. 265.

July 16th. To examine ourselves is good; but useless unless we also examine Environment. To bewail our weakness is right, but not remedial. The cause must be investigated as well as the result. And yet, because we never see the other half of the problem, our failures even fail to instruct us. After each new collapse we begin our life anew, but on the old conditions; and the attempt ends as usual in the repetition--in the circumstances the inevitable repetition--of the old disaster. Natural Law, Environment, p. 265.

July 17th. After seasons of much discouragement, with the sore sense upon us of our abject feebleness, we do confer with ourselves, insisting for the thousandth time, "My soul, wait thou only upon God." But, the lesson is soon forgotten. The strength supplied we speedily credit to our own achievement; and even the temporary success is mistaken for a symptom of improved inward vitality. Once more we become self-existent. Once more we go on living without an Environment. And once more, after days of wasting without repairing, of spending without replenishing, we begin to perish with hunger, only returning to God again, as a last resort, when we have reached starvation point. Natural Law, Environment, p. 266.

July 18th. Why this unscientific attempt to sustain life for weeks at a time without an Environment? It is because we have never truly seen the necessity for an Environment. We have not been working with a principle. We are told to "wait only upon God," but we do not know why. It has never been as clear to us that without God the soul will die as that without food the body will perish. In short, we have never comprehended the doctrine of the Persistence of Force. Instead of being content to transform energy we have tried to create it. Natural Law, Environment, p. 266.

July 19th. Whatever energy the soul expends must first be "taken into it from without." We are not Creators, but creatures; God is our refuge AND STRENGTH. Communion with God, therefore, is a scientific necessity; and nothing will more help the defeated spirit which is struggling in the wreck of its religious life than a common-sense hold of this biological principle that without Environment he can do nothing. Natural Law, Environment, p. 267.

July 20th. Who has not come to the conclusion that he is but a part, a fraction of some larger whole? Who does not miss, at every turn of his life, an absent God? That man is but a part, he knows, for there is room in him for more. That God is the other part, he feels, because at times He satisfies his need. Who does not tremble often under that sicklier symptom of his incompleteness, his want of spiritual energy, his helplessness with sin? But now he understands both--the void in his life, the powerlessness of his will. He understands that, like all other energy, Spiritual power is contained in Environment. He finds here at last the true root of all human frailty, emptiness, nothingness, sin. This is why "without Me ye can do nothing." Powerlessness is the normal state, not only of this, but of every organism--of every organism apart from its Environment. Natural Law, p. 268.

July 21st. Friendship is the nearest thing we know to what religion is. God is love. And to make religion akin to Friendship is simply to give it the highest expression conceivable by man. The Changed Life, p. 49.

July 22d. The entire dependence of the soul upon God is not an exceptional mystery, nor is man's helplessness an arbitrary and unprecedented phenomenon. It is the law of all Nature. The spiritual man is not taxed beyond the natural. He is not purposely handicapped by singular limitations or unusual incapacities. God has not designedly made the religious life as hard as possible. The arrangements for the spiritual life are the same as for the natural life. When, in their hours of unbelief, men challenge their Creator for placing the obstacle of human frailty in the way of their highest development, their protest is against the order of Nature. Natural Law, p. 269.

July 23d. The organism must either depend on his environment, or be self-sufficient. But who will not rather approve the arrangement by which man in his creatural life may have unbroken access to an Infinite Power? What soul will seek to remain self-luminous when it knows that "The Lord God is a Sun?" Who will not willingly exchange his shallow vessel for Christ's well of living water. Natural Law, p. 270.

July 24th. The New Testament is nowhere more impressive than where it insists on the fact of man's dependence. In its view the first step in religion is for man to feel his helplessness. Christ's first beatitude is to the poor in spirit. The condition of entrance into the spiritual kingdom is to possess the child-spirit--that state of mind combining at once the profoundest helplessness with the most artless feeling of dependence. Natural Law, p. 271.

July 25th. Fruit-bearing without Christ is not an improbability, but an impossibility. As well expect the natural fruit to flourish without air and heat, without soil and sunshine. How thoroughly also Paul grasped this truth is apparent from a hundred pregnant passages in which he echoes his Master's teaching. To him life was hid with Christ in God. And that he embraced this, not as a theory but as an experimental truth, we gather from his constant confession, "When I am weak, then am I strong." Natural Law, p. 271.

July 26th. One result of the due apprehension of our personal helplessness will be that we shall no longer waste our time over the impossible task of manufacturing energy for ourselves. Our science will bring to an abrupt end the long series of severe experiments in which we have indulged in the hope of finding a perpetual motion. And having decided upon this once for all, our first step in seeking a more satisfactory state of things must be to find a new source of energy. Following Nature, only one course is open to us. We must refer to Environment. The natural life owes all to Environment, so must the spiritual. Now the Environment of the spiritual life is God. As Nature, therefore, forms the complement of the natural life. God is the complement of the spiritual. Natural Law, p. 272.

July 27th. Do not think that nothing is happening because you do not see yourself grow, or hear the whirr of the machinery. All great things grow noiselessly. You can see a mushroom grow, but never a child. Mr. Darwin tells us that Evolution proceeds by "numerous, successive, and slight modifications." The Changed Life, p. 54.

July 28th. We fail to praise the ceaseless ministry of the great inanimate world around us only because its kindness is unobtrusive. Nature is always noiseless. All her greatest gifts are given in secret. And we forget how truly every good and perfect gift comes from without, and from above, because no pause in her changeless beneficence teaches us the sad lessons of deprivation. Natural Law, p. 274.

July 29th. It is not a strange thing for the soul to find its life in God. This is its native air. God as the Environment of the soul has been from the remotest age the doctrine of all the deepest thinkers in religion. How profoundly Hebrew poetry is saturated with this high thought will appear when we try to conceive of it with this left out. Natural Law, p. 374.

July 30th. The alternatives of the intellectual life are

Christianity or Agnosticism. The Agnostic is right when he trumpets his incompleteness. He who is not complete in Him must be for ever incomplete. Natural Law, p. 278.

July 31st. The problems of the heart and conscience are infinitely more perplexing than those of the intellect. Has love no future? Has right no triumph? Is the unfinished self to remain unfinished? The alternatives are two, Christianity or Pessimism. But when we ascend the further height of the religious nature, the crisis comes. There, without Environment, the darkness is unutterable. So maddening now becomes the mystery that men are compelled to construct an Environment for themselves. No Environment here is unthinkable. An altar of some sort men must have-- God, or Nature, or Law. But the anguish of Atheism is only a negative proof of man's incompleteness. Natural Law, p. 279.

August 1st. A photograph prints from the negative only while exposed to the sun. While the artist is looking to see how it is getting on he simply stops the getting on. Whatever of wise supervision the soul may need, it is certain it can never be over-exposed, or that, being exposed, anything else in the world can improve the result or quicken it. The Changed Life, pp. 56, 57.

August 2d. What a very strange thing, is it not, for man to pray? It is the symbol at once of his littleness and of his greatness. Here the sense of imperfection, controlled and silenced in the narrower reaches of his being, becomes audible. Now he must utter himself. The sense of need is so real, and the sense of Environment, that he calls out to it, addressing it articulately, and imploring it to satisfy his need. Surely there is nothing more touching in Nature than this? Man could never so expose himself, so break through all constraint, except from a dire necessity. Natural Law, p. 279.

August 3d. What is Truth? The natural Environment answers, "Increase of Knowledge increaseth Sorrow," and "much study is a Weariness." Christ replies, "Learn of Me, and ye shall find Rest." Contrast the world's word "Weariness" with Christ's word "Rest." No other teacher since the world began has ever associated "learn" with "Rest." Learn of me, says the philosopher, and you shall find Restlessness. Learn of Me, says Christ, and ye shall find Rest. Natural Law, p. 280.

August 4th. Men will have to give up the experiment of attempting to live in half an Environment. Half an Environment will give but half a Life.... He whose correspondences are with this world alone has only a thousandth part, a fraction, the mere rim and shade of an Environment, and only the fraction of a Life. How long will it take Science to believe its own creed, that the material universe we see around us is only a fragment of the universe we do not see? Natural Law, p. 282.

August 5th. The Life of the senses, high and low, may perfect itself in Nature. Even the Life of thought may find a large complement in surrounding things. But the higher thought, and the conscience, and the religious Life, can only perfect themselves in God. Natural Law, p. 283.

August 6th. To make the influence of Environment stop

with the natural world is to doom the spiritual nature to death. For the soul, like the body, can never perfect itself in isolation. The law for both is to be complete in the appropriate Environment. Natural Law, p. 283.

August 7th. Take into your new sphere of labour, where you also mean to lay down your life, that simple charm, Love, and your life-work must succeed. You can take nothing greater, you need take nothing less. It is not worth while going if you take anything less. The Greatest Thing in the World, p. 17.

August 8th. Politeness has been defined as love in trifles. Courtesy is said to be love in little things. And the one secret of politeness is to love. Love CANNOT behave itself unseemly. You can put the most untutored persons into the highest society, and if they have a reservoir of Love in their heart, they will not behave themselves unseemly. They simply cannot do it. The Greatest Thing in the World, p. 26.

August 9th. I believe that Christ's yoke is easy. Christ's "yoke" is just His way of taking life. And I believe it is an easier way than any other. I believe it is a happier way than any other. The most obvious lesson in Christ's teaching is that there is no happiness in having and getting anything, but only in giving. The Greatest Thing in the World, p. 29.

August 10th. Half the world is on the wrong scent in the pursuit of happiness. They think it consists in having and getting, and in being served by others. It consists in giving, and in serving others. He that would be great among you, said Christ, let him serve. He that would be happy, let him remember that there is but one way--it is more blessed, it is more happy, to give than to receive. The Greatest Thing in the World, p. 30.

August 11th. "Love is not easily provoked." . . . We are inclined to look upon bad temper as a very harmless weakness. We speak of it as a mere infirmity of nature, a family failing, a matter of temperament, not a thing to take into very serious account in estimating a man's character. And yet here, right in the heart of this analysis of love, it finds a place; and the Bible again and again returns to condemn it as one of the most destructive elements in human nature. The Greatest Thing in the World, p. 30.

August 12th. The peculiarity of ill-temper is that it is the vice of the virtuous. It is often the one blot on an otherwise noble character. You know men who are all but perfect, and women who would be entirely perfect, but for an easily ruffled, quick-tempered, or "touchy" disposition. This compatibility of ill-temper with high moral character is one of the strangest and saddest problems of ethics. The Greatest Thing in the World, p. 31.

August 13th. What makes a man a good artist, a good sculptor, a good musician? Practice. . . . What makes a man a good man? Practice. Nothing else. There is nothing capricious about religion. We do not get the soul in different ways, under different laws, from those in which we get the body and the mind. The Greatest Thing in the World, p. 40.

August 14th. Love is not a thing of enthusiastic emotion. It is a rich, strong, manly, vigorous expression of the whole round Christian character--the Christ-like nature in its fullest development. And the constituents of this great character are only to be built up by ceaseless practice. The Greatest Thing in the World, p. 41.

August 15th. We know but little now about the conditions of the life that is to come. But what is certain is that Love must last. God, the Eternal God, is Love. Covet, therefore, that everlasting gift. The Greatest Thing in the World, p. 54.

August 16th. To love abundantly is to live abundantly, and to love forever is to live forever. Hence, eternal life is inextricably bound up with love. . . . Love must be eternal. It is what God is. The Greatest Thing in the World, pp. 57, 58.

August 17th. When a man becomes a Christian the natural process is this: The Living Christ enters into his soul. Development begins. The quickening Life seizes upon the soul, assimilates surrounding elements, and begins to fashion it. According to the great Law of Conformity to Type this fashioning takes a specific form. It is that of the Artist who fashions. And all through Life this wonderful, mystical, glorious, yet perfectly definite, process, goes on "until Christ be formed" in it. Natural Law, p. 294.

August 18th. The Christian Life is not a vague effort after righteousness--an ill-defined, pointless struggle for an ill-defined, pointless end. Religion is no dishevelled mass of aspiration, prayer, and faith. There is no more mystery in Religion as to its processes than in Biology. Natural Law, p. 294.

August 19th. There is much mystery in Biology. "We know all but nothing of Life" yet, nothing of development. There is the same mystery in the spiritual Life. But the great lines are the same, as decided, as luminous; and the laws of natural and spiritual are the same, as unerring, as simple. Will everything else in the natural world unfold its order, and yield to Science more and more a vision of harmony, and Religion, which should complement and perfect all, remain a chaos? Natural Law, p. 294.

August 20th. When one attempts to sanctify himself by effort, he is trying to make his boat go by pushing against the mast. He is like a drowning man trying to lift himself out of the water by pulling at the hair of his own head. Christ held up this method almost to ridicule when He said: "Which of you by taking thought can add a cubit to his stature?" The one redeeming feature of the self-sufficient method is this--that those who try it find out almost at once that it will not gain the goal. The Changed Life, p. 11.

August 21st. The Image of Christ that is forming within us--that is life's one charge. Let every project stand aside for that. "Till Christ be formed," no man's work is finished, no religion crowned, no life has fulfilled its end. The Changed Life, p. 62.

August 22d. Our companionship with Him, like all true companionship, is a spiritual communion. All friendship, all love, human and Divine, is purely spiritual. It was after He was risen that He influenced even the disciples most. The Changed Life, p. 38.

August 23d. Make Christ your most constant companion. Be more under His influence than under any other influence. Ten minutes spent in His society every day, ay, two minutes if it be face to face, and heart to heart, will make the whole day different. Every character has an inward spring, let Christ be it. Every action has a key-note, let Christ set it. The Changed Life, p. 40.

August 24th. Under the right conditions it is as natural for character to become beautiful as for a flower; and if on God's earth there is not some machinery for effecting it, the supreme gift to the world has been forgotten. This is simply what man was made for. With Browning: "I say that Man was made to grow, not stop." The Changed Life, p. 10.

August 25th. How can modern men today make Christ, the absent Christ, their most constant companion still? The answer is that Friendship is a spiritual thing. It is independent of Matter, or Space, or Time. That which I love in my friend is not that which I see. What influences me in my friend is not his body but his spirit. The Changed Life, p. 37.

August 26th. Love should be the supreme thing--because it is going to last; because in the nature of things it is an Eternal Life. It is a thing that we are living now, not that we get when we die; that we shall have a poor chance of getting when we die unless we are living now. The Greatest Thing in the World, p. 58.

August 27th. When will it be seen that the characteristic of the Christian Religion is its Life, that a true theology must begin with a Biology? Theology is the Science of God. Why will men treat God as inorganic? Natural Law, p. 297.

August 28th. We should be forsaking the lines of nature were we to imagine for a moment that the new creature was to be formed out of nothing. Nothing can be made out of nothing. Matter is uncreatable and indestructible; Nature and man can only form and transform. Hence when a new animal is made, no new clay is made. Life merely enters into already existing matter, assimilates more of the same sort and rebuilds it. The spiritual Artist works in the same way. He must have a peculiar kind of protoplasm, a basis of life, and that must be already existing. Natural Law, p. 297.

August 29th. However active the intellectual or moral life may be, from the point of view of this other Life it is dead. That which is flesh is flesh. It wants, that is to say, the kind of Life which constitutes the difference between the Christian and the not-a-Christian, It has not yet been "born of the Spirit." Natural Law, p. 299.

August 30th. The protoplasm in man has a something in addition to its instincts or its habits. It has a capacity for God. In this capacity for God lies its receptivity; it is the very protoplasm that was necessary. The chamber is not only ready to receive the new Life, but the Guest is expected, and, till He comes, is missed. Till then the soul longs and yearns, wastes and pines, waving its tentacles piteously in the empty air, feeling after God if so be that it may find Him. This is not peculiar to the protoplasm of the Christian's soul. In every land and in every age there have been altars to the Known or Unknown God. Natural Law, p. 300.

August 31st. It is now agreed as a mere question of anthropology that the universal language of the human soul has always been "I perish with hunger." This is what fits it for Christ. There is a grandeur in this cry from the depths which makes its very unhappiness sublime. Natural Law, p. 300.

September 1st. In reflecting the character of Christ, it is no real obstacle that we may never have been in visible contact with Himself. Many men know Dante better than their own fathers. He influences them more. As a spiritual presence he is more near to them, as a spiritual force more real. Is there any reason why a greater than ... Dante should not also instruct, inspire, and mould the characters of men? The Changed Life, pp. 38, 52.

September 2d. Mark this distinction. . . . Imitation is mechanical, reflection organic. The one is occasional, the other habitual. In the one case, man comes to God and imitates Him; in the other, God comes to man and imprints Himself upon him. It is quite true that there is an imitation of Christ which amounts to reflection. But Paul's term includes all that the other holds, and is open to no mistake. "Whom having not seen, I love." The Changed Life, p. 39.

September 3d. In paraphrase: We all reflecting as a mirror the character of Christ are transformed into the same Image from character to character--from a poor character to a better one, from a better one to one a little better still, from that to one still more complete, until by slow degrees the Perfect Image is attained. Here the solution of the problem of sanctification is compressed into a sentence: Reflect the character of Christ and you will become like Christ. The Changed Life, p. 24.

September 4th. Not more certain is it that it is something outside the thermometer that produces a change in the thermometer, than it is something outside the soul of man that produces a moral change upon him. That he must be susceptible to that change, that he must be a party to it, goes without saying; but that neither his aptitude nor his will can produce it is equally certain. The Changed Life, p. 20.

September 5th. Just as in an organism we have these three things-- formative matter, formed matter, and the forming principle or life; so in the soul we have the old nature, the renewed nature, and. the transforming Life. Natural Law, p. 302.

September 6th. Is it hopeless to point out that one of the most recognizable characteristics of life is its unrecognizableness, and that the very token of its spiritual nature lies in its being beyond the grossness of our eyes? Natural Law, p. 302.

September 7th. According to the doctrine of Bio-genesis, life can only come from life. It was Christ's additional claim that His function in the world, was to give men Life. "I am come that ye might have Life, and that ye might have it more abundantly." This could, not refer to the natural life, for men had that already. He that hath the Son hath another Life. "Know ye not your own selves how that Jesus Christ is in you." Natural Law, p. 303.

September 8th. The recognition of the Ideal is the first step in the direction of Conformity. But let it be clearly observed that it is but a step. There is no vital connection between merely seeing the Ideal and being conformed to it. Thousands admire Christ who never become Christians. Natural Law, p. 306.

September 9th. For centuries men have striven to find out ways and means to conform themselves to the Christ Life. Impressive motives have been pictured, the proper circumstances arranged, the direction of effort defined, and men have toiled, struggled, and agonized to conform themselves to the Image of the Son. Can the protoplasm CONFORM ITSELF to its type? Can the embryo FASHION ITSELF? Is Conformity to Type produced by the matter OR BY THE LIFE, by the protoplasm or by the Type? Is organization the cause of life or the effect of it? It is the effect of it. Conformity to Type, therefore, is secured by the type. Christ makes the Christian. Natural Law, p. 307.

September 10th. O preposterous and vain man, thou who couldest not make a fingernail of thy body, thinkest thou to fashion this wonderful, mysterious, subtle soul of thine after the ineffable Image? Wilt thou ever permit thyself TO BE conformed to the Image of the Son? Wilt thou, who canst not add a cubit to thy stature, submit TO BE raised by the Type-Life within thee to the perfect stature of Christ Natural Law, p. 308.

September 11th. Men will still experiment "by works of righteousness which they have done" to earn the Ideal life. The doctrine of Human Inability, as the Church calls it, has always been objectionable to men who do not know themselves. Natural Law, p. 309.

September 12th. Let man choose Life; let him daily nourish his soul; let him forever starve the old life; let him abide continuously as a living branch in the Vine, and the True-Vine Life will flow into his soul, assimilating, renewing, conforming to Type, till Christ, pledged by His own law, be formed in him. Natural Law, p. 312.

September 13th. The work begun by Nature is finished by the Supernatural --as we are wont to call the higher natural. And as the veil is lifted by Christianity it strikes men dumb with wonder. For the goal of Evolution is Jesus Christ. Natural Law, p. 314.

September 14th. The Christian life is the only life that will ever be completed. Apart from Christ the life of man is a broken pillar, the race of men an unfinished pyramid. One by one in sight of Eternity all human Ideals fall short, one by one before the open grave all human hopes dissolve. Natural Law, p. 314.

September 15th. I do not think we ourselves are aware how much our religious life is made up of phrases; how much of what we call Christian experience is only a dialect of the Churches, a mere religious phraseology with almost nothing behind it in what we really feel and know. Pax Vobiscum, p. 12.

September 16th. The ceaseless chagrin of a self-centred life can be removed at once by learning Meekness and Lowliness of heart. He who learns them is forever proof against it. He lives henceforth a charmed life. Pax Vobiscum, p. 29.

September 17th. Great trials come at lengthened intervals, and we rise to breast them; but it is the petty friction of our everyday life with one another, the jar of business or of work, the discord of the domestic circle, the collapse of our ambition, the crossing of our will or the taking down of our conceit, which makes inward peace impossible. Pax Vobiscum, p. 28.

September 18th. There are people who go about the world looking out for slights, and they are necessarily miserable, for they find them at every turn--especially the imaginary ones. One has the same pity for such men as for the very poor. They are the morally illiterate. They have had no real education, for they have never learned how to live. Pax Vobiscum, p. 31.

September 19th. Christ never said much in mere words about the Christian graces. He lived them, He was them. Yet we do not merely copy Him. We learn His art by living with Him. Pax Vobiscum, p. 32.

September 20th. Christ's invitation to the weary and heavy-laden is a call to begin life over again upon a new principle--upon His own principle. "Watch My way of doing things," He says. "Follow Me. Take life as I take it. Be meek and lowly, and you will find Rest." Pax Vobiscum, p. 32.

September 21st. If a man could make himself humble

to order, it might simplify matters, but we do not find that this happens. Hence we must all go through the mill. Hence death, death to the lower self, is the nearest gate and the quickest road to life. Pax Vobiscum, p. 35.

September 22d. Whatever rest is provided by Christianity for the children of God, it is certainly never contemplated that it should supersede personal effort. And any rest which ministers to indifference is immoral and unreal--it makes parasites and not men. Natural Law, p. 335.

September 23d. Just because God worketh in him, as the evidence and triumph of it, the true child of God works out his own salvation--works it out having really received it--not as a light thing, a superfluous labour, but with fear and trembling as a reasonable and indispensable service. Natural Law, p. 335.

September 24th. Christianity, as Christ taught, is the truest philosophy of life ever spoken. But let us be quite sure when we speak of Christianity, that we mean Christ's Christianity. Pax Vobiscum, p. 47.

September 25th. So far from ministering to growth, parasitism ministers to decay. So far from ministering to holiness, that is to wholeness, parasitism ministers to exactly the opposite. One by one the spiritual faculties droop and die, one by one from lack of exercise the muscles of the soul grow weak and flaccid, one by one the moral activities cease. So from him that hath not, is taken away that which he hath, and after a few years of parasitism there is nothing left to save. Natural Law, p. 336.

September 26th. The natural life, not less than the eternal, is the gift of God. But life in either case is the beginning of growth and not the end of grace. To pause where we should begin, to retrograde where we should advance, to seek a mechanical security that we may cover inertia and find a wholesale salvation in which there is no personal sanctification--this is Parasitism. Natural Law, p. 336.

September 27th. Could we investigate the spirit as a living organism, or study the soul of the backslider on principles of comparative anatomy, we should have a revelation of the organic effects of sin, even of the mere sin of carelessness as to growth and work, which must revolutionize our ideas of practical religion. There is no room for the doubt even that what goes on in the body does not with equal certainty take place in the spirit under the corresponding conditions. Natural Law, p. 345.

September 28th. It is the beautiful work of Christianity everywhere to adjust the burden of life to those who bear it, and them to it. It has a perfectly miraculous gift of healing. Without doing any violence to human nature it sets it right with life, harmonizing it with all surrounding things, and restoring those who are jaded with the fatigue and dust of the world to a new grace of living. Pax Vobiscum, p. 46.

September 29th. The penalty of backsliding is not something unreal and vague, some unknown quantity which may be measured out to us disproportionately, or which, perchance, since God is good, we may altogether evade. The consequences are already marked within the structure of the soul. So to speak, they are physiological. The thing effected by our in difference or by our indulgence is not the book of final judgment, but the present fabric of the soul. Natural Law, p. 346.

September 30th. The punishment of degeneration is simply degeneration-- the loss of functions, the decay of organs, the atrophy of the spiritual nature. It is well known that the recovery of the backslider is one of the hardest problems in spiritual work. To reinvigorate an old organ seems more difficult and hopeless than to develop a new one; and the backslider's terrible lot is to have to retrace with enfeebled feet each step of the way along which he strayed; to make up inch by inch the leeway he has lost, carrying with him a dead-weight of acquired reluctance, and scarce knowing whether to be stimulated or discouraged by the oppressive memory of the previous fall. Natural Law, p. 346.

October 1st. He who abandons the personal search for truth, under whatever pretext, abandons truth. The very word truth, by becoming the limited possession of a guild, ceases to have any meaning; and faith, which can only be founded on truth, gives way to credulity, resting on mere opinion. Natural Law, p. 352.

October 2d. It is more necessary for us to be active than to be orthodox. To be orthodox is what we wish to be, but we can only truly reach it by being honest, by being original, by seeing with our own eyes, by believing with our own heart. Natural Law. p. 364.

October 3d. Better a little faith dearly won, better launched alone on the infinite bewilderment of Truth, than perish on the splendid plenty of the richest creeds. Such Doubt is no self-willed presumption. Nor, truly exercised, will it prove itself, as much doubt does, the synonym for sorrow. Natural Law, p. 365.

October 4th. Christianity removes the attraction of the earth; and this is one way in which it diminishes men's burden. It makes them citizens of another world. Pax Vobiscum, p. 47.

October 5th. Then the Christian experiences are our own making? In the same sense in which grapes are our own making, and no more. All fruits GROW--whether they grow in the soil or in the soul; whether they are the fruits of the wild grape or of the True Vine. No man can MAKE things grow. He can GET THEM TO GROW by arranging all the circumstances and fulfilling all the conditions. But the growing is done by God. Pax Vobiscum, p. 56.

October 6th. Men may not know how fruits grow, but they do know that they cannot grow in five minutes. Some lives have not even a stalk on which fruits could hang, even if they did grow in five minutes. Some have never planted one sound seed of Joy in all their lives; and others who may have planted a germ or two have lived so little in sunshine that they never could come to maturity. Pax Vobiscum, p. 51.

October 7th. There is no mystery about Happiness whatever. Put in the right ingredients and it must come out. He that abideth in Him will bring forth much fruit;

and bringing forth much fruit is Happiness. The infallible receipt for Happiness, then, is to do good; and the infallible receipt for doing good is to abide in Christ. Pax Vobiscum, p. 56.

October 8th. Spend the time you have spent in sighing for fruits in fulfilling the conditions of their growth. The fruits will come, must come. . . . About every other method of living the Christian life there is an uncertainty. About every other method of acquiring the Christian experiences there is a "perhaps." But in so far as this method is the way of nature, it cannot fail. Pax Vobiscum, p. 58.

October 9th. The distinctions drawn between men are commonly based on the outward appearance of goodness or badness, on the ground of moral beauty or moral deformity--is this classification scientific? Or is there a deeper distinction between the Christian and the not-a-Christian as fundamental as that between the organic and the inorganic? Natural Law, p. 374.

October 10th What is the essential difference between the Christian and the not-a-Christian, between the spiritual beauty and the moral beauty? It is the distinction between the Organic and the Inorganic. Moral beauty is the product of the natural man, spiritual beauty of the spiritual man. Natural Law, p. 380.

October 11th. The first Law of biology is: That which is Mineral is Mineral; that which is Flesh is Flesh; that which is Spirit is Spirit. The mineral remains in the inorganic world until it is seized upon by a something called Life outside the inorganic world; the natural man remains the natural man, until a Spiritual Life from without the natural life seizes upon him, regenerates him, changes him into a spiritual man. Natural Law, p. 381.

October 12th Suppose now it be granted for a moment that the character of the not-a-Christian is as beautiful as that of the Christian. This is simply to say that the crystal is as beautiful as the organism. One is quite entitled to hold this; but what he is not entitled to hold is that both in the same sense are living. "He that hath the Son hath Life, and he that hath not the Son of God hath not Life." Natural Law, p. 382.

October 13th. Man is a moral animal, and can, and ought to, arrive at great natural beauty of character. But this is simply to obey the law of his nature--the law of his flesh; and no progress along that line can project him into the spiritual sphere. Natural Law, p. 382.

October 14th. If any one choose to claim that the mineral beauty, the fleshly beauty, the natural moral beauty, is all he covets, he is entitled to his claim. To be good and true, pure and benevolent in the moral sphere, are high and, so far, legitimate objects in life. If he deliberately stop here, he is at liberty to do so. But what he is not entitled to do is to call himself a Christian, or to claim to discharge the functions peculiar to the Christian life. Natural Law, p. 382.

October 15th. In dealing with a man of fine moral character, we are dealing with the highest achievement of the organic kingdom. But in dealing with a spiritual man we are dealing with THE LOWEST FORM OF LIFE IN

THE SPIRITUAL WORLD. To contrast the two, therefore, and marvel that the one is apparently so little better than the other, is unscientific and unjust. Natural Law, p. 385.

October 16th. The spiritual man is a mere unformed embryo, hidden as yet in his earthly chrysalis-case, while the natural man has the breeding and evolution of ages represented in his character. But what are the possibilities of this spiritual organism? What is yet to emerge from this chrysalis-case? The natural character finds its limits within the organic sphere. But who is to define the limits of the spiritual? Even now it is very beautiful. Even as an embryo it contains some prophecy of its future glory. But the point to mark is, that "it doth not yet appear what it shall be." Natural Law, p. 386.

October 17th. The best test for Life is just LIVING. And living consists, as we have formerly seen, in corresponding with Environment. Those therefore who find within themselves, and regularly exercise, the faculties for corresponding with the Divine Environment, may be said to live the Spiritual Life. Natural Law, p. 390.

October 18th. That the Spiritual Life, even in the embryonic organism, ought already to betray itself to others, is certainly what one would expect. Every organism has its own reaction upon Nature, and the reaction of the spiritual organism upon the community must be looked for. In the absence of any such reaction, in the absence of any token that it lived for a higher purpose, or that its real interests were those of the Kingdom to which it professed to belong, we should be entitled to question its being in that Kingdom. Natural Law, p. 390.

October 19th. Man's place in Nature, or his position among the Kingdoms, is to be decided by the characteristic functions habitually discharged by him. Now, when the habits of certain individuals are closely observed, when the total effect of their life and work, with regard to the community, is gauged, . . . there ought to be no difficulty in deciding whether they are living for the Organic or for the Spiritual; in plainer language, for the world or for God. Natural Law, p. 391.

October 20th. No matter what may be the moral uprightness of man's life, the honourableness of his career, or the orthodoxy of his creed, if he exercises the function of loving the world, that defines his world--he belongs to the Organic Kingdom. He cannot in that case belong to the higher Kingdom. "If any man love the world, the love of the Father is not in him." After all, it is by the general bent of a man's life, by his heart-impulses and secret desires, his spontaneous actions and abiding motives, that his generation is declared. Natural Law, p. 393.

October 21st. The imperious claim of a Kingdom upon its members is not peculiar to Christianity. It is the law in all departments of Nature that every organism must live for its Kingdom. And in defining living FOR the higher Kingdom as the condition of living in it, Christ enunciates a principle which all Nature has prepared us to expect. Natural Law, p. 395.

October 22d. Christianity marks the advent of what is simply a new Kingdom. Its distinctions from the Kingdom below it are fundamental. It demands from its members activities and responses of an altogether novel order. It is, in the conception of its Founder, a Kingdom for which all its adherents must henceforth exclusively live and work, and which opens its gates alone upon those who, having counted the cost, are prepared to follow it if need be to the death. The surrender Christ demanded was absolute. Every aspirant for membership must seek FIRST the Kingdom of God. Natural Law, p. 394.

October 23d. Until even religious men see the uniqueness of Christ's society, until they acknowledge to the full extent its claim to be nothing less than a new Kingdom, they will continue the hopeless attempt to live for two Kingdoms at once. And hence the value of a more explicit Classification. For probably the most of the difficulties of trying to live the Christian life arise from attempting to half-live it. Natural Law, p. 396.

October 24th. Two Kingdoms, at the present time, are known to Science-- the Inorganic and the Organic. The spiritual life does not belong to the Inorganic Kingdom, because it lives. It does not belong to the Organic Kingdom, because it is endowed with a kind of Life infinitely removed from either the vegetable or animal. Where, then, shall it be classed? We are left without an alternative. There being no Kingdom known to Science which can contain it, we must construct one. Or, rather, we must include in the programme of Science a Kingdom already constructed, but the place of which in Science has not yet been recognized. That Kingdom is the KINGDOM OF

GOD. Natural Law, p. 397.

October 25th. The goal of the organisms of the Spiritual World is nothing less than this--to be "holy as He is holy, and pure as He is pure." And by the Law of Conformity to Type, their final perfection is secured. The inward nature must develop out according to its Type, until the consummation of oneness with God is reached. Natural Law, p. 403.

October 26th. Christianity defines the highest conceivable future for mankind. It satisfies the Law of Continuity. It guarantees the necessary conditions for carrying on the organism successfully, from stage to stage. It provides against the tendency to Degeneration. And finally, instead of limiting the yearning hope of final perfection to the organisms of a future age--an age so remote that the hope for thousands of years must still be hopeless--instead of inflicting this cruelty on intelligences mature enough to know perfection and earnest enough to wish it, Christianity puts the prize within immediate reach of man. Natural Law, p. 404.

October 27th. No worse fate can befall a man in this world than to live and grow old alone, unloving and unloved. To be lost is to live in an unregenerate condition, loveless and unloved; and to be saved is to love; he that dwelleth in love dwelleth already in God. For God is Love. The Greatest Thing in the World, p. 59.

October 28th. "Love suffereth long, and is kind; love envieth not; love vaunteth not itself." Get these ingredients into your life. Then everything that you do is eternal.

It is worth doing. It is worth giving time to. The Greatest Thing in the World, p. 60.

October 29th. The final test of religion at that great Day is not religiousness, but Love; not what I have done, not what I have believed, not what I have achieved, but how I have discharged the common charities of life. The Greatest Thing in the World, p. 62.

October 30th. The words which all of us shall one Day hear sound not of theology but of life, not of churches and saints, but of the hungry and the poor, not of creeds and doctrines, but of shelter and clothing, not of Bibles and prayer-books, but of cups of cold water in the name of Christ. The Greatest Thing in the World, p. 63.

October 31st. The world moves. And each day, each hour, demands a further motion and re-adjustment for the soul. A telescope in an observatory follows a star by clockwork, but the clockwork of the soul is called the Will. Hence, while the soul in passivity reflects the Image of the Lord, the Will in intense activity holds the mirror in position lest the drifting motion of the world bear it beyond the line of vision. To "follow Christ" is largely to keep the soul in such position as will allow for the motion of the earth. And this calculated counteracting of the movements of a world, this holding of the mirror exactly opposite to the Mirrored, this steadying of the faculties unerringly, through cloud and earthquake; fire and sword, is the stupendous cooperating labour of the Will. The Changed Life, p. 60.

November 1st. All around us Christians are wearing

themselves out in trying to be better. The amount of spiritual longing in the world--in the hearts of unnumbered thousands of men and women in whom we should never suspect it; among the wise and thoughtful; among the young and gay, who seldom assuage and never betray their thirst--this is one of the most wonderful and touching facts of life. It is not more heat that is needed, but more light; not more force, but a wiser direction to be given to very real energies already there. Pax Vobiscum, p. 14.

November 2d. Men sigh for the wings of a dove, that they may fly away and be at Rest. But flying away will not help us. "The Kingdom of God is WITHIN YOU." We aspire to the top to look for Rest; it lies at the bottom. Water rests only when it gets to the lowest place. So do men. Hence, be lowly. Pax Vobiscum, p. 30.

November 3d. The kingdom of God is righteousness, peace, joy. Righteousness, of course, is just doing what is right. Any boy who does what is right has the kingdom of God within him. Any boy who, instead of being quarrelsome, lives at peace with the other boys, has the kingdom of God within him. Any boy whose heart is filled with joy because he does what is right, has the kingdom of God within him. The kingdom of God is not going to religious meetings, and hearing strange religious experiences: the kingdom of God is doing what is right--living at peace with all men, being filled with joy in the Holy Ghost. First, p. 11.

November 4th. The man who has no opinion of himself at all can never be hurt if others do not acknowledge him. Hence, be meek. He who is without expectation cannot fret if nothing comes to him. It is self-evident that these things are so. The lowly man and the meek man are really above all other men, above all other things. Pax Vobiscum, p. 30.

November 5th. Keep religion in its place, and it will take you straight through life, and straight to your Father in heaven when life is over. But if you do not put it in its place, you may just as well have nothing to do with it. Religion out of its place in a human life is the most miserable thing in the world. There is nothing that requires so much to be kept in its place as religion, and its place is what? second? third? "First." Boys, carry that home with you today--FIRST the kingdom of God. Make it so that it will be natural to you to think about that the very first thing. First, pp. 15, 16.

November 6th. The change we have been striving after is not to be produced by any more striving after. It is to be wrought upon us by the moulding of hands beyond our own. As the branch ascends, and the bud bursts, and the fruit reddens under the cooperation of influences from the outside air, so man rises to the higher stature under invisible pressures from without. The Changed Life, p. 21.

November 7th. Every man's character remains as it is, or continues in the direction in which it is going, until it is compelled by IMPRESSED FORCES to change that state. Our failure has been the failure to put ourselves in the way of the impressed forces. There is a clay, and there is a Potter; we have tried to get the clay to mould the clay. The

Changed Life, p. 21.

November 8th. Character is a unity, and all the virtues must advance together to make the perfect man. This method of sanctification, nevertheless, is in the true direction. It is only in the details of execution that it fails. The Changed Life, p. 14.

November 9th. We all reflecting as a mirror the character of Christ are transformed into the same Image from character to character--from a poor character to a better one, from a better one to one a little better still, from that to one still more complete, until by slow degrees the Perfect Image is attained. Here the solution of the problem of sanctification is compressed into a sentence: Reflect the character of Christ, and you will become like Christ. The Changed Life, p. 24.

November 10th. There are some men and some women in whose company we are always at our best. While with them we cannot think mean thoughts or speak ungenerous words. Their mere presence is elevation, purification, sanctity. All the best stops in our nature are drawn out by their intercourse, and we find a music in our souls that was never there before. The Changed Life, p. 33.

November 11th. Take such a sentence as this: African explorers are subject to fevers which cause restlessness and delirium. Note the expression, "cause restlessness." RESTLESSNESS HAS A CAUSE. Clearly, then, any one who wished to get rid of restlessness would proceed at once to deal with the cause. Pax Vobiscum, p. 20.

November 12th. What Christian experience wants is

THREAD, a vertebral column, method. It is impossible to believe that there is no remedy for its unevenness and dishevelment, or that the remedy is a secret. The idea, also, that some few men, by happy chance or happier temperament, have been given the secret--as if there were some sort of knack or trick of it--is wholly incredible. Religion must ripen fruit for every temperament; and the way even into its highest heights must be by a gateway through which the peoples of the world may pass. Pax Vobiscum, p. 15.

November 13th. Nothing that happens in the world happens by chance. God is a God of order. Everything is arranged upon definite principles, and never at random. The world, even the religious world, is governed by law. Character is governed by law. Happiness is governed by law. The Christian experiences are governed by law. Pax Vobiscum, p. 17.

November 14th. We ARE CHANGED, as the Old Version has it--we do not change ourselves. No man can change himself. Throughout the New Testament you will find that wherever these moral and spiritual transformations are described the verbs are in the passive. Presently it will be pointed out that there is a rationale in this; but meantime do not toss these words aside as if this passivity denied all human effort or ignored intelligible law. What is implied for the soul here is no more than is everywhere claimed for the body. The Changed Life, p. 19.

November 15th. Rain and snow do drop from the air, but not without a long previous history. They are the mature effects of former causes. Equally so are Rest, and Peace, and Joy. They, too, have each a previous history. Storms and winds and calms are not accidents, but are brought about by antecedent circumstances. Rest and Peace are but calms in man's inward nature, and arise through causes as definite and as inevitable. Pax Vobiscum, p. 18.

November 16th. Few men know how to live. We grow up at random, carrying into mature life the merely animal methods and motives which we had as little children. And it does not occur to us that all this must be changed; that much of it must be reversed; that life is the finest of the Fine Arts; that it has to be learned with life-long patience, and that the years of our pilgrimage are all too short to master it triumphantly. Pax Vobiscum, p. 31.

November 17th. Christ's life outwardly was one of the most troubled lives that was ever lived: Tempest and tumult, tumult and tempest, the waves breaking over it all the time till the worn body was laid in the grave. But the inner life was a sea of glass. The great calm was always there. At any moment you might have gone to Him and found Rest. Pax Vobiscum, p. 35.

November 18th. The creation of a new heart, the renewing of a right spirit is an omnipotent work of God. Leave it to the Creator. "He which hath begun a good work in you will perfect it unto that day." The Changed Life, p. 57.

November 19th. To become like Christ is the only thing in the world worth caring for, the thing before which every ambition of man is folly, and all lower achievement vain. Those only who make this quest the supreme desire and passion of their lives can even begin to hope to reach it. The Changed Life, p. 57.

November 20th. A religion of effortless adoration may be a religion for an angel but never for a man. Not in the contemplative, but in the active, lies true hope; not in rapture, but in reality, lies true life; not in the realm of ideals, but among tangible things, is man's sanctification wrought. The Changed Life, p. 58.

November 21st. Nothing ever for a moment broke the serenity of Christ's life on earth. Misfortune could not reach Him; He had no fortune. Food, raiment, money--fountain-heads of half the world's weariness--He simply did not care for; they played no part in His life; He "took no thought" for them. It was impossible to affect Him by lowering His reputation; He had already made Himself of no reputation. He was dumb before insult. When He was reviled, He reviled not again. In fact, there was nothing that the world could do to Him that could ruffle the surface of His spirit. Pax Vobiscum, p. 36.

November 22d. Life is the cradle of eternity. As the man is to the animal in the slowness of his evolution, so is the spiritual man to the natural man. Foundations which have to bear the weight of an eternal life must be surely laid. Character is to wear forever; who will wonder or grudge that it cannot be developed in a day? The Changed Life, p. 55.

November 23d. To await the growing of a soul is an almost Divine act of faith. How pardonable, surely, the impatience of deformity with itself, of a consciously despicable character standing before Christ, wondering, yearning, hungering to be like that? Yet must one trust the process fearlessly, and without misgiving. "The Lord the Spirit" will do His part. The tempting expedient is, in haste for abrupt or visible progress, to try some method less spiritual, or to defeat the end by watching for effects instead of keeping the eye on the Cause. The Changed Life, p. 56.

November 24th. The Image of Christ that is forming within us--that is life's one charge. Let every project stand aside for that. "Till Christ be formed," no man's work is finished, no religion crowned, no life has fulfilled its end. Is the infinite task begun? When, how, are we to be different? Time cannot change men. Death cannot change men. Christ can. Wherefore PUT ON CHRIST. The Changed Life, p. 62.

November 25th. Christ saw that men took life painfully. To some it was a weariness, to others a failure, to many a tragedy, to all a struggle and a pain. How to carry this burden of life had been the whole world's problem. It is still the whole world's problem. And here is Christ's solution. "Carry it as I do. Take life as I take it. Look at it from My point of view. Interpret it upon My principles. Take My yoke and learn of Me, and you will find it easy. For My yoke is easy, works easily, sits right upon the shoulders, and THEREFORE My burden is light." Pax Vobiscum, p. 44.

November 26th. There is a disease called "touchiness"--a disease which, in spite of its innocent name, is one of the gravest sources of restlessness in the world. Touchiness, when it becomes chronic, is a morbid condition of the inward disposition. It is self-love inflamed to the acute point. . . The cure is to shift the yoke to some other place; to let men and things touch us through some new and perhaps as yet unused part of our nature; to become meek and lowly in heart while the old nature is becoming numb from want of use. Pax Vobiscum, pp. 45, 46.

November 27th. Christ's yoke is simply His secret for the alleviation of human life, His prescription for the best and happiest method of living. Men harness themselves to the work and stress of the world in clumsy and unnatural ways. The harness they put on is antiquated. A rough, ill-fitted collar at the best, they make its strain and friction past enduring, by placing it where the neck is most sensitive; and by mere continuous irritation this sensitiveness increases until the whole nature is quick and sore. Pax Vobiscum, p. 45.

November 28th. No one can get Joy by merely asking for it. It is one of the ripest fruits of the Christian life, and, like all fruits, must be grown. Pax Vobiscum, p. 50.

November 29th Christ is the source of Joy to men in the sense in which He is the source of Rest. His people share His life, and therefore share its consequences, and one of these is Joy. His method of living is one that in the nature of things produces Joy. When He spoke of His Joy remaining with us He meant in part that the causes which produced it should continue to act. His followers, that is to say, by repeating His life would experience its accompaniments. His Joy, His kind of Joy, would remain with them. Pax Vobiscum, p. 54.

November 30th. Think of it, the past is not only focussed there, in a man's soul, it IS there. How could it be reflected from there if it were not there? All things that he has ever seen, known, felt, believed of the surrounding world are now within him, have become part of him, in part are him--he has been changed into their image. He may deny it, he may resent it, but they are there. They do not adhere to him, they are transfused through him. He cannot alter or rub them out. They are not in his memory, they are in HIM. His soul is as they have filled it, made it, left it. The Changed Life, p. 27.

December 1st. Temper is significant, not in what it is alone but in what it reveals. . . . It is a test for love, a symptom, a revelation of an unloving nature at bottom. It is the intermittent fever which bespeaks unintermittent disease within; the occasional bubble escaping to the surface which betrays some rottenness underneath; a sample of the most hidden products of the soul dropped involuntarily when off one's guard; IN A WORD, the lightning form of a hundred hideous and un-Christian sins. The Greatest Thing in the World, p. 34.

December 2d. You will find, as you look back upon your life, that the moments that stand out, the moments when you have really lived, are the moments when you have done things in a spirit of love. As memory scans the past, above and beyond all the transitory pleasures of life there leap forward those supreme hours when you have been enabled to do unnoticed kindnesses to those round about you, things too trifling to speak about, but which you feel have entered into your eternal life. The Greatest Thing in the World, p. 60.

December 3d. If events change men, much more persons. No man can meet another on the street without making some mark upon him. We say we exchange words when we meet; what we exchange is souls. And when intercourse is very close and very frequent, so complete is this exchange that recognizable bits of the one soul begin to show in the other's nature, and the second is conscious of a similar and growing debt to the first. The Changed Life, p. 30.

December 4th. In the natural world we absorb heat, breathe air, draw on Environment all but automatically for meat and drink, for the nourishment of the senses, for mental stimulus, for all that, penetrating us from without, can prolong, enrich, and elevate life. But in the spiritual world we have all this to learn. We are new creatures, and even the bare living has to be acquired. Natural Law, p. 267.

December 5th. The great point in learning to live the spiritual life is to live naturally. As closely as possible we must follow the broad, clear lines of the natural life. And there are three things especially which it is necessary for us to keep continually in view. The first is that the organism contains within itself only one-half of what is essential to life; the second is that the other half is contained in the Environment; the third, that the condition of receptivity is simple union between the organism and the Environment. Natural Law, p. 268.

December 6th. To say that the organism contains within itself only one-half of what is essential to life, is to repeat the evangelical confession, so worn and yet so true to universal experience, of the utter helplessness of man. Natural Law, p. 268.

December 7th. Who has not come to the conclusion that he is but a part, a fraction of some larger whole? Who does not miss at every turn of his life an absent God? That man is but a part, he knows, for there is room in him for more. That God is the other part, he feels, because at times He satisfies his need. Who does not tremble often under that sicklier symptom of his incompleteness, his want of spiritual energy, his helplessness with sin? But now he understands both--the void in his life, the powerlessness of his will. He understands that, like all other energy, spiritual power is contained in Environment. He finds here at last the true root of all human frailty, emptiness, nothingness, sin. This is why "without Me ye can do nothing." Powerless is the normal state not only of this but of every organism--of every organism apart from its Environment. Natural Law, p. 268.

December 8th. To seize continuously the opportunity of more and more perfect adjustment to better and higher conditions, to balance some inward evil with some purer influence acting from without, in a word to make our Environment at the same time that it is making us-- these are the secrets of a well-ordered and successful life. Natural Law, p. 256.

December 9th. In the spiritual world the subtle influences which form and transform the soul are Heredity and Environment. And here especially, where all is invisible, where much that we feel to be real is yet so ill-defined, it becomes of vital practical moment to clarify the atmosphere as far as possible with conceptions borrowed from the natural life. Natural Law, p. 256.

December 10th. These lower correspondences are in their nature unfitted for an Eternal Life. Even if they were perfect in their relation to their Environment, they would still not be Eternal. However opposed, apparently, to the scientific definition of Eternal Life, it is yet true that perfect correspondence with Environment is not Eternal Life. . . . An Eternal Life demands an Eternal Environment. Natural Law, p. 245.

December 11th. On what does the Christian argument for Immortality really rest? It stands upon the pedestal on which the theologian rests the whole of historical Christianity--the Resurrection of Jesus Christ. Natural Law, p. 234.

December 12th. The soul which has no correspondence with the spiritual environment is spiritually dead. It may be that it never possessed . . . the spiritual ear, or a heart which throbbed in response to the love of God. If so, having never lived, it cannot be said to have died. But not to have these correspondences is to be in the state of Death. To the spiritual world, to the Divine Environment, it is dead--as a stone which has never lived is dead to the environment of the organic world. Natural Law, p. 177.

December 13th. The humanity of what is called "sud-

den conversion" has never been insisted on as it deserves.
...While growth is a slow and gradual process, the change
from Death to Life, alike in the natural and spiritual spheres,
is the work of the moment. Whatever the conscious hour
of the second birth may be--in the case of an adult it is
probably defined by the first real victory over sin--it is
certain that on biological principles the real turning-point
is literally a moment. Natural Law, p. 184.

December 14th. Christ says we must hate life. Now,
this does not apply to all life. It is "life in this world" that
is to be hated. For life in this world implies conformity to
this world. It may not mean pursuing worldly pleasures, or
mixing with worldly sets; but a subtler thing than that--a
silent deference to worldly opinion; an almost unconscious
lowering of religious tone to the level of the worldly-re-
ligious world around; a subdued resistance to the soul's
delicate promptings to greater consecration, out of deference to "breadth" or fear of ridicule. These, and such
things, are what Christ tells us we must hate. For these
things are of the very essence of worldliness. "If any man
love the world," even in this sense, "the love of the Father
is not in him." Natural Law, p. 197.

December 15th. To correspond with the God of Science, the Eternal Unknowable, would be everlasting existence; to correspond with "the true God and Jesus Christ,"
is Eternal Life. The quality of the Eternal Life alone makes
the heaven; mere everlastingness might be no boon. Even
the brief span of the temporal life is too long for those
who spend its years in sorrow. Natural Law, p. 220.

December 16th. The relation between the spiritual man and his Environment is, in theological language, a filial relation. With the new Spirit, the filial correspondence, he knows the Father--and this is Life Eternal. This is not only the real relation, but the only possible relation: "Neither knoweth any man the Father save the Son, and he to whomsoever the Son will reveal Him." And this on purely natural grounds. Natural Law, p. 229.

December 17th. Communion with God--can it be demonstrated in terms of Science that this is a correspondence which will never break? We do not appeal to Science for such a testimony. We have asked for its conception of an Eternal Life; and we have received for answer that Eternal Life would consist in a correspondence which should never cease, with an Environment which should never pass away. And yet what would Science demand of a perfect correspondence that is not met by this, THE KNOWING OF GOD? There is no other correspondence which could satisfy one at least of the conditions. Not one could be named which would not bear on the face of it the mark and pledge of its mortality. But this, to know God, stands alone. Natural Law, p. 220.

December 18th. The misgiving which will creep sometimes over the brightest faith has already received its expression and its rebuke: "Who shall separate us from the love of Christ? Shall tribulation, or distress, or persecution, or famine, or nakedness, or peril, or sword?" Shall these "changes in the physical state of the environment" which threaten death to the natural man, destroy the spiritual?

Shall death, or life, or angels, or principalities, or powers, arrest or tamper with his eternal correspondences? "Nay, in all these things we are more than conquerors through Him that loved us. For I am persuaded that neither death, nor life, nor angels, nor principalities, nor powers, nor things present, nor things to come, nor height, nor depth, nor any other creature, shall be able to separate us from the love of God, which is in Christ Jesus our Lord." Rom. viii, 35-39. Natural Law, p. 230.

December 19th. "We find that man, or the spiritual man, is equipped with two sets of correspondences." One set possesses the quality of everlastingness, the other is temporal. But unless these are separated by some means the temporal will continue to impair and hinder the eternal. The final preparation, therefore, for the inheriting of Eternal Life must consist in the abandonment of the non-eternal elements. These must be unloosed and dissociated from the higher elements. And this is effected by a closing catastrophe--Death. Natural Law, p. 248.

December 20th. Heredity and Environment are the master-influences of the organic world. These have made all of us what we are. These forces are still ceaselessly playing upon all our lives. And he who truly understands these influences; he who has decided how much to allow to each; he who can regulate new forces as they arise, or adjust them to the old, so directing them as at one moment to make them cooperate, at another to counter act one another, understands the rationale of personal development. Natural Law, p. 255.

December 21st. It is the Law of Influence that WE BECOME LIKE THOSE WHOM WE HABITUALLY ADMIRE. Through all the range of literature, of history, and biography this law presides. Men are all mosaics of other men. There was a savour of David about Jonathan and a savour of Jonathan about David. Jean Valjean, in the masterpiece of Victor Hugo, is Bishop Bienvenu risen from the dead. Metempsychosis is a fact. The Changed Life, p. 31.

December 22d. Can we shut our eyes to the fact that the religious opinions of mankind are in a state of flux? And when we regard the uncertainty of current beliefs, the war of creeds, the havoc of inevitable as well as of idle doubt, the reluctant abandonment of early faith by those who would cherish it longer if they could, is it not plain that the one thing thinking men are waiting for is the introduction of Law among the Phenomena of the Spiritual World? When that comes we shall offer to such men a truly scientific theology. And the Reign of Law will transform the whole Spiritual World as it has already transformed the Natural World. Natural Law, Preface, p. ix.

December 23d. We have Truth in Nature as it came from God. And it has to be read with the same unbiassed mind, the same open eye, the same faith, and the same reverence as all other Revelation. All that is found there, whatever its place in Theology, whatever its orthodoxy or heterodoxy, whatever its narrowness or its breadth, we are bound to accept as Doctrine from which on the lines of Science there is no escape. Natural Law, Preface, p. xi.

December 24th. In Nature generally, we come upon

new Laws as we pass from lower to higher kingdoms, the old still remaining in force, the newer Laws which one would expect to meet in the Spiritual World would so transcend and overwhelm the older as to make the analogy or identity, even if traced, of no practical use. The new Laws would represent operations and energies so different, and so much more elevated, that they would afford the true keys to the Spiritual World. Natural Law, p. 47.

December 25th. The visible is the ladder up to the invisible; the temporal is but the scaffolding of the eternal. And when the last immaterial souls have climbed through this material to God, the scaffolding shall be taken down, and the earth dissolved with fervent heat--not because it was base, but because its work is done. Natural Law, p. 57.

December 26th. The natural man belongs essentially to this present order of things. He is endowed simply with a high quality of the natural animal Life. But it is Life of so poor a quality that it is not Life at all. He that hath not the Son hath not Life; but he that hath the Son hath Life-- a new and distinct and supernatural endowment. He is not of this world. He is of the timeless state, of Eternity. IT DOTH NOT YET APPEAR WHAT HE SHALL BE. Natural Law, p. 82.

December 27th. The gradualness of growth is a characteristic which strikes the simplest observer. Long before the word Evolution was coined Christ applied it in this very connection--"First the blade, then the ear, then the full corn in the ear." It is well known also to those who study the parables of Nature that there is an ascending scale of slowness as we rise in the scale of Life. Growth is most gradual in the highest forms. Man attains his maturity after a score of years; the monad completes its humble cycle in a day. What wonder if development be tardy in the Creature of Eternity? A Christian's sun has sometimes set, and a critical world has seen as yet no corn in the ear. As yet? "As yet," in this long Life, has not begun. Grant him the years proportionate to his place in the scale of Life. "The time of harvest is NOT YET." Natural Law, p. 92.

December 28th. Salvation is a definite process. If a man refuse to submit himself to that process, clearly he cannot have the benefits of it. "As many as received Him to them gave He power to become the sons of God." He does not avail himself of this power. It may be mere carelessness or apathy. Nevertheless the neglect is fatal. He cannot escape because he will not. Natural Law, p. 109.

December 29th. The end of Salvation is perfection, the Christ-like mind, character, and life. Morality is on the way to this perfection; it may go a considerable distance toward it, but it can never reach it. Only Life can do that. . . . Morality can never reach perfection; Life MUST. For the Life must develop out according to its type; and being a germ of the Christ-life, it must unfold into A CHRIST. Natural Law, p. 138.

December 30th. Perfect life is not merely the possessing of perfect functions, but of perfect functions perfectly adjusted to each other, and all conspiring to a single result, the perfect working of the whole organism. It is not said that the character will develop in all its fulness in this life. That were a time too short for an Evolution so magnificent. In this world only the cornless ear is seen: sometimes only the small yet still prophetic blade. Natural Law, p. 129.

December 31st. The immortal soul must give itself to something that is immortal. And the only immortal things are these: "Now abideth faith, hope, love, but the greatest of these is love." Some think the time may come when two of these three things will also pass away--faith into sight, hope into fruition. Paul does not say so. We know but little now about the conditions of the life that is to come. But what is certain is that Love must last. God, the Eternal God, is Love. Covet therefore that everlasting gift. The Greatest Thing in the World, pp. 54, 55.

The Codes Of Hammurabi And Moses
W. W. Davies

QTY

The discovery of the Hammurabi Code is one of the greatest achievements of archaeology, and is of paramount interest, not only to the student of the Bible, but also to all those interested in ancient history...

Religion   **ISBN:** *1-59462-338-4*   **Pages:132**
MSRP $12.95

The Theory of Moral Sentiments
Adam Smith

QTY

This work from 1749. contains original theories of conscience amd moral judgment and it is the foundation for systemof morals.

Philosophy   **ISBN:** *1-59462-777-0*   **Pages:536**
MSRP $19.95

Jessica's First Prayer
Hesba Stretton

QTY

In a screened and secluded corner of one of the many railway-bridges which span the streets of London there could be seen a few years ago, from five o'clock every morning until half past eight, a tidily set-out coffee-stall, consisting of a trestle and board, upon which stood two large tin cans, with a small fire of charcoal burning under each so as to keep the coffee boiling during the early hours of the morning when the work-people were thronging into the city on their way to their daily toil...

Childrens   **ISBN:** *1-59462-373-2*   **Pages:84**
MSRP $9.95

My Life and Work
Henry Ford

QTY

Henry Ford revolutionized the world with his implementation of mass production for the Model T automobile. Gain valuable business insight into his life and work with his own auto-biography... "We have only started on our development of our country we have not as yet, with all our talk of wonderful progress, done more than scratch the surface. The progress has been wonderful enough but..."

Biographies/   **ISBN:** *1-59462-198-5*   **Pages:300**
MSRP $21.95

The Art of Cross-Examination
Francis Wellman

QTY

I presume it is the experience of every author, after his first book is published upon an important subject, to be almost overwhelmed with a wealth of ideas and illustrations which could readily have been included in his book, and which to his own mind, at least, seem to make a second edition inevitable. Such certainly was the case with me; and when the first edition had reached its sixth impression in five months, I rejoiced to learn that it seemed to my publishers that the book had met with a sufficiently favorable reception to justify a second and considerably enlarged edition. ..

Pages:412

Reference   **ISBN:** *1-59462-647-2*   *MSRP $19.95*

On the Duty of Civil Disobedience
Henry David Thoreau

QTY

Thoreau wrote his famous essay, On the Duty of Civil Disobedience, as a protest against an unjust but popular war and the immoral but popular institution of slave-owning. He did more than write—he declined to pay his taxes, and was hauled off to gaol in consequence. Who can say how much this refusal of his hastened the end of the war and of slavery ?

Law   **ISBN:** *1-59462-747-9*   **Pages:48**

MSRP $7.45

Dream Psychology Psychoanalysis for Beginners
Sigmund Freud

QTY

Sigmund Freud, born Sigismund Schlomo Freud (May 6, 1856 - September 23, 1939), was a Jewish-Austrian neurologist and psychiatrist who co-founded the psychoanalytic school of psychology. Freud is best known for his theories of the unconscious mind, especially involving the mechanism of repression; his redefinition of sexual desire as mobile and directed towards a wide variety of objects; and his therapeutic techniques, especially his understanding of transference in the therapeutic relationship and the presumed value of dreams as sources of insight into unconscious desires.

Pages:196

Psychology   **ISBN:** *1-59462-905-6*   *MSRP $15.45*

The Miracle of Right Thought
Orison Swett Marden

QTY

Believe with all of your heart that you will do what you were made to do. When the mind has once formed the habit of holding cheerful, happy, prosperous pictures, it will not be easy to form the opposite habit. It does not matter how improbable or how far away this realization may see, or how dark the prospects may be, if we visualize them as best we can, as vividly as possible, hold tenaciously to them and vigorously struggle to attain them, they will gradually become actualized, realized in the life. But a desire, a longing without endeavor, a yearning abandoned or held indifferently will vanish without realization.

Pages:360

Self Help   **ISBN:** *1-59462-644-8*   *MSRP $25.45*

QTY

☐ **The Rosicrucian Cosmo-Conception Mystic Christianity** by *Max Heindel*   ISBN: *1-59462-188-8*   **$38.95**
The Rosicrucian Cosmo-conception is not dogmatic, neither does it appeal to any other authority than the reason of the student. It is: not controversial, but is: sent forth in the, hope that it may help to clear..   New Age/Religion Pages 646

☐ **Abandonment To Divine Providence** by *Jean-Pierre de Caussade*   ISBN: *1-59462-228-0*   **$25.95**
"The Rev. Jean Pierre de Caussade was one of the most remarkable spiritual writers of the Society of Jesus in France in the 18th Century. His death took place at Toulouse in 1751. His works have gone through many editions and have been republished...   Inspirational/Religion Pages 400

☐ **Mental Chemistry** by *Charles Haanel*   ISBN: *1-59462-192-6*   **$23.95**
Mental Chemistry allows the change of material conditions by combining and appropriately utilizing the power of the mind. Much like applied chemistry creates something new and unique out of careful combinations of chemicals the mastery of mental chemistry...   New Age Pages 354

☐ **The Letters of Robert Browning and Elizabeth Barret Barrett 1845-1846 vol II**   ISBN: *1-59462-193-4*   **$35.95**
by *Robert Browning and Elizabeth Barrett*   Biographies Pages 596

☐ **Gleanings In Genesis (volume I)** by *Arthur W. Pink*   ISBN: *1-59462-130-6*   **$27.45**
Appropriately has Genesis been termed "the seed plot of the Bible" for in it we have, in germ form, almost all of the great doctrines which are afterwards fully developed in the books of Scripture which follow...   Religion/Inspirational Pages 420

☐ **The Master Key** by *L. W. de Laurence*   ISBN: *1-59462-001-6*   **$30.95**
In no branch of human knowledge has there been a more lively increase of the spirit of research during the past few years than in the study of Psychology, Concentration and Mental Discipline. The requests for authentic lessons in Thought Control, Mental Discipline and...   New Age/Business Pages 422

☐ **The Lesser Key Of Solomon Goetia** by *L. W. de Laurence*   ISBN: *1-59462-092-X*   **$9.95**
This translation of the first book of the "Lernegton" which is now for the first time made accessible to students of Talismanic Magic was done, after careful collation and edition, from numerous Ancient Manuscripts in Hebrew, Latin, and French...   New Age/Occult Pages 92

☐ **Rubaiyat Of Omar Khayyam** by *Edward Fitzgerald*   ISBN: *1-59462-332-5*   **$13.95**
Edward Fitzgerald, whom the world has already learned, in spite of his own efforts to remain within the shadow of anonymity, to look upon as one of the rarest poets of the century, was born at Bredfield, in Suffolk, on the 31st of March, 1809. He was the third son of John Purcell...   Music Pages 172

☐ **Ancient Law** by *Henry Maine*   ISBN: *1-59462-128-4*   **$29.95**
The chief object of the following pages is to indicate some of the earliest ideas of mankind, as they are reflected in Ancient Law, and to point out the relation of those ideas to modern thought.   Religion/History Pages 452

☐ **Far-Away Stories** by *William J. Locke*   ISBN: *1-59462-129-2*   **$19.45**
"Good wine needs no bush, but a collection of mixed vintages does. And this book is just such a collection. Some of the stories I do not want to remain buried for ever in the museum files of dead magazine-numbers an author's not unpardonable vanity..."   Fiction Pages 272

☐ **Life of David Crockett** by *David Crockett*   ISBN: *1-59462-250-7*   **$27.45**
"Colonel David Crockett was one of the most remarkable men of the times in which he lived. Born in humble life, but gifted with a strong will, an indomitable courage, and unremitting perseverance..   Biographies/New Age Pages 424

☐ **Lip-Reading** by *Edward Nitchie*   ISBN: *1-59462-206-X*   **$25.95**
Edward B. Nitchie, founder of the New York School for the Hard of Hearing, now the Nitchie School of Lip-Reading, Inc, wrote "LIP-READING Principles and Practice". The development and perfecting of this meritorious work on lip-reading was an undertaking...   How-to Pages 400

☐ **A Handbook of Suggestive Therapeutics, Applied Hypnotism, Psychic Science**   ISBN: *1-59462-214-0*   **$24.95**
by *Henry Munro*   Health/New Age/Health/Self-help Pages 376

☐ **A Doll's House: and Two Other Plays** by *Henrik Ibsen*   ISBN: *1-59462-112-8*   **$19.95**
Henrik Ibsen created this classic when in revolutionary 1848 Rome. Introducing some striking concepts in playwriting for the realist genre, this play has been studied the world over.   Fiction/Classics/Plays 308

☐ **The Light of Asia** by *sir Edwin Arnold*   ISBN: *1-59462-204-3*   **$13.95**
In this poetic masterpiece, Edwin Arnold describes the life and teachings of Buddha. The man who was to become known as Buddha to the world was born as Prince Gautama of India but he rejected the worldly riches and abandoned the reigns of power when... Religion/History/Biographies Pages 170

☐ **The Complete Works of Guy de Maupassant** by *Guy de Maupassant*   ISBN: *1-59462-157-8*   **$16.95**
"For days and days, nights and nights, I had dreamed of that first kiss which was to consecrate our engagement, and I knew not on what spot I should put my lips..."   Fiction/Classics Pages 240

☐ **The Art of Cross-Examination** by *Francis L. Wellman*   ISBN: *1-59462-309-0*   **$26.95**
Written by a renowned trial lawyer, Wellman imparts his experience and uses case studies to explain how to use psychology to extract desired information through questioning.   How-to/Science/Reference Pages 408

☐ **Answered or Unanswered?** by *Louisa Vaughan*   ISBN: *1-59462-248-5*   **$10.95**
Miracles of Faith in China   Religion Pages 112

☐ **The Edinburgh Lectures on Mental Science (1909)** by *Thomas*   ISBN: *1-59462-008-3*   **$11.95**
This book contains the substance of a course of lectures recently given by the writer in the Queen Street Hall, Edinburgh. Its purpose is to indicate the Natural Principles governing the relation between Mental Action and Material Conditions...   New Age/Psychology Pages 148

☐ **Ayesha** by *H. Rider Haggard*   ISBN: *1-59462-301-5*   **$24.95**
Verily and indeed it is the unexpected that happens! Probably if there was one person upon the earth from whom the Editor of this, and of a certain previous history, did not expect to hear again...   Classics Pages 380

☐ **Ayala's Angel** by *Anthony Trollope*   ISBN: *1-59462-352-X*   **$29.95**
The two girls were both pretty, but Lucy who was twenty-one who supposed to be simple and comparatively unattractive, whereas Ayala was credited, as her Bombwhat romantic name might show, with poetic charm and a taste for romance. Ayala when her father died was nineteen...   Fiction Pages 484

☐ **The American Commonwealth** by *James Bryce*   ISBN: *1-59462-286-8*   **$34.45**
An interpretation of American democratic political theory. It examines political mechanics and society from the perspective of Scotsman James Bryce   Politics Pages 572

☐ **Stories of the Pilgrims** by *Margaret P. Pumphrey*   ISBN: *1-59462-116-0*   **$17.95**
This book explores pilgrims religious oppression in England as well as their escape to Holland and eventual crossing to America on the Mayflower, and their early days in New England...   History Pages 268

www.bookjungle.com *email: sales@bookjungle.com fax: 630-214-0564 mail: Book Jungle PO Box 2226 Champaign, IL 61825*

QTY

The Fasting Cure *by Sinclair Upton*
ISBN: *1-59462-222-1* **$13.95**

In the Cosmopolitan Magazine for May, 1910, and in the Contemporary Review (London) for April, 1910, I published an article dealing with my experiences in fasting. I have written a great many magazine articles, but never one which attracted so much attention... New Age/Self Help/Health Pages 164

Hebrew Astrology *by Sepharial*
ISBN: *1-59462-308-2* **$13.45**

In these days of advanced thinking it is a matter of common observation that we have left many of the old landmarks behind and that we are now pressing forward to greater heights and to a wider horizon than that which represented the mind-content of our progenitors... Astrology Pages 144

Thought Vibration or The Law of Attraction in the Thought World
by William Walker Atkinson
ISBN: *1-59462-127-6* **$12.95**

Psychology/Religion Pages 144

Optimism *by Helen Keller*
ISBN: *1-59462-108-X* **$15.95**

Helen Keller was blind, deaf, and mute since 19 months old, yet famously learned how to overcome these handicaps, communicate with the world, and spread her lectures promoting optimism. An inspiring read for everyone... Biographies/Inspirational Pages 84

Sara Crewe *by Frances Burnett*
ISBN: *1-59462-360-0* **$9.45**

In the first place, Miss Minchin lived in London. Her home was a large, dull, tall one, in a large, dull square, where all the houses were alike, and all the sparrows were alike, and where all the door-knockers made which same heavy sound... Childrens/Classic Pages 88

The Autobiography of Benjamin Franklin *by Benjamin Franklin*
ISBN: *1-59462-135-7* **$24.95**

The Autobiography of Benjamin Franklin has probably been more extensively read than any other American historical work, and no other book of its kind has had such ups and downs of fortune. Franklin lived for many years in England, where he was agent... Biographies/History Pages 332

Name	
Email	
Telephone	
Address	
City, State ZIP	

☐ **Credit Card**   ☐ **Check / Money Order**

Credit Card Number	
Expiration Date	
Signature	

Please Mail to: Book Jungle
PO Box 2226
Champaign, IL 61825
or Fax to: 630-214-0564

ORDERING INFORMATION
web: *www.bookjungle.com*
email: *sales@bookjungle.com*
fax: *630-214-0564*
mail: *Book Jungle PO Box 2226 Champaign, IL 61825*
or PayPal *to sales@bookjungle.com*

Please contact us for bulk discounts

DIRECT-ORDER TERMS

**20% Discount if You Order
Two or More Books**
Free Domestic Shipping!
Accepted: Master Card, Visa,
Discover, American Express

Printed in the United States
98981LV00005B/49/A